Meal Finder

Detox Your Body and DASH

June Craig and Maryanne Lane

Copyright © 2013 June Craig and Maryanne Lane
All rights reserved.

Table of Contents

INTRODUCTION 1

SECTION 1: DETOX RECIPES 6

CHAPTER 1: WHAT IS THE DETOX DIET? 7

CHAPTER 2: BENEFITS OF DETOXIFYING 9

CHAPTER 3: HELPFUL TIPS FOR DETOX DIET SUCCESS 12

Before You Go on a Detox Diet – Helpful Preparation Tips 12

What Should You Eat? 14

What You Should NOT Eat 17

Foods that Offer the Best Detoxification Punch 19

CHAPTER 4: DETOX DIET BREAKFAST RECIPES 21
    Detox Friendly Buckwheat Pancakes 21
    Vegetarian Breakfast Patty Recipe 23
    Easy Herbed Egg Omelet Recipe 25
    Seedy Almond Spread Recipe 27
    Apple Nut Oatmeal Recipe 29
    Homemade Apple Cinnamon Granola Recipe 31
    Date Porridge Recipe 33

CHAPTER 5: DETOX DIET SOUP AND SALAD RECIPES 35
    Detox Minestrone Soup Recipe 35
    Gazpacho Soup Recipe 37
    Delicious Lemon Dressed Kale Salad Recipe 39

Tuscan Veggie Bean Soup Recipe 41
Grapefruit and Sesame Salad Recipe 43
Miso Soup Recipe 44
Cleansing Seaweed Salad Recipe 46
Easy Black Bean Chili Recipe 48

CHAPTER 6: SIDE DISH DETOX RECIPES 50
Tasty Roasted Roots Recipe 50
Burdock Carrot Stir Fry Recipe 52
Easy Spinach and Cabbage Pie Recipe 54

CHAPTER 7: MAIN DISH DETOX DIET RECIPES 57
Vegetarian Black Bean Burgers Recipe 57
Red Snapper and Kale Recipe 60
Tasty Green Leaf Lettuce Wraps Recipe 62
Salmon Fillets with Orange Glaze Recipe 64
Wild Rice and Chicken Recipe 66
Scallop and Leek Risotto Recipe 68
Lemon Rosemary Chicken Recipe 70
Easy Stir Fried Veggies and Fish Recipe 72
Lemon Ginger Braised Shrimp Recipe 74

CHAPTER 8: DETOX DRINK AND DETOX SMOOTHIE RECIPES 76
Delicious Strawberry Smoothie Recipe 76
Delicious Green Cleansing Juice Recipe 78
Tropical Pineapple Smoothie 79
Cacao Powder Smoothie Recipe 80
Tasty Berry Juice Recipe 82
Easy Orange Yogurt Smoothie Recipe 84

CHAPTER 9: DETOX DIET SNACK AND APPETIZER RECIPES 85
Easy Mint Salsa Recipe 85
Seed and Nut Veggie Dip Recipe 87
Crispy, Healthy Kale Chip Recipe 89
Coconut Chocolate Homemade Energy Bars 91

CHAPTER 10: DETOX DIET DESSERT RECIPES 93
Homemade Chocolate Pudding Recipe 93
Detox Pumpkin Pie Recipe 95
Easy Natural Fudge (No Sugar) Recipe 97
Delicious Peach Bake Dessert Recipe 99
Poached Honeyed Pears Recipe 101

CHAPTER 11: DETOX DIET 7 DAY MEAL PLAN 103

SECTION 2: DASH DIET 109

WHAT IS THE DASH DIET? 110
What Is Hypertension and Why Is It Dangerous? 111
How Does the DASH Diet Work? 112

DASH STUDY DAILY NUTRIENT GOALS 114

DASH DIET GUIDELINES 115
Using DASH for Weight Loss 116
Intuitive Eating with the DASH Diet 116
Making DASH Dieting Easy 117

EXERCISE AND THE DASH DIET 119

RECIPES FOR THE DASH DIET 120
Appetizers 121
    DASH Spinach Dip 121
    Stuffed Portabella Mushrooms 123
    Crispy Coconut Chicken Fingers 125
    Vegetable Sushi 127
    Fresh Mushroom Quesadillas 129

Beverages 131
   Peanut Butter and Banana Smoothie 131
   No-Booze Margarita 132
   Sugar-free Agua Fresca 133
   Spicy, Sweet and Tangy Herbal Tea 135
   Non-Alcoholic Hurricane Punch 136

Breakfast 137
   Chewy Fruit Bars 137
   Broiled Almond-Banana Toast 139
   DASH-friendly Oatmeal 140
   Healthy Homemade Granola 141
   Toasted Breakfast Sandwich 143

Main Dishes 145
   Simple Grilled Chicken 145
   Basic Barbeque "Pork" Chops 146
   Miso-Marinated Cod 148
   Blackened Beef 150
   Feta-ricotta Greek Pizza 152
   Chinese Restaurant Ginger Beef 154
   Vegetable Medley Pasta Sauce 156
   Portabella Mushroom "Burgers" 158

Sides 160
   Baked Macaroni and Cheese 160
   Spicy Steamed Eggplant with Peanut Sauce 162
   Braised Spring Vegetables 164
   Rice Pilaf with Saffron 166
   Spicy Garlic Green Beans 168

Salads 170
   Spicy Tuna Salad 170
   Tabbouleh with Tomatoes 171
   Edamame Salad 173
   Raw Okra Salad 175
   Tomato-Zucchini Salad with Eggs 177
   Low Cholesterol Potato Salad 179

Soups 181
   Nutrient-packed Kale Soup 181

Meatless Lentil Chili 184
Tangy Carrot Curry 186
Cream of Wild Rice Soup with Fennel 188
Hearty Turkey Soup 190

DASH DIET 5-DAY SAMPLE MENU 192

Modifying the 5-Day Meal Plan 195

CONCLUSION 196

Introduction

Are you like most people who struggle to figure out what's for dinner? It sometimes seems an impossible task for someone who has no idea what to prepare and especially so if the goal for the meal is to eat healthier? In this book you need not struggle any longer with figuring out how to find a good healthy meal. The recipes within this book are set to give you the best ingredients featuring healthy whole foods including fruits, vegetables, and lean proteins. You don't even have to struggle with snacks and desserts because you can find good recipes here that will make for great snack time.

Why choose a healthy lifestyle? It can seem like it's easier just to eat convenient foods, but in the long run it isn't easier on your health. Many people will forgo eating healthy just because it complicates meal planning and preparing. They do not know where to start or what to prepare. Eating healthier means letting go of junk foods and all those processed convenient foods. It means grabbing onto the old art of homemade cooking. But homemade cooking can also be junk foods. This is where Meal Finder will help you to figure out your meal plans offering healthy foods from both the detox diet and the DASH diet plans.

The detox diet plan helps to set a body up for being healthier by promoting the detoxification of germs and toxins that we get from the environment and from eating the wrong foods. Certain foods help to scrub the body from the inside out. The diet serves to cleanse the liver, kidneys, digestive system, and even the blood. The detox diet is a perfect companion to the DASH diet.

The DASH diet is also called the hypertension or the high blood pressure diet. This diet specifically helps people to naturally lower their blood pressure. It was originally a diet that was prescribed with patients with hypertension, but now it's a healthy diet that anyone can eat. Because the DASH diet uses foods that are naturally good to lower blood pressure, they are foods that are healthy for the entire cardiovascular system. If these foods help to lower high blood pressure they also help to maintain normal blood pressure and everyone needs that.

A healthy lifestyle starts with a good diet. If you can maintain a healthy lifestyle you will help your body to stay well. There is nothing better for prevention that to start with the foods you eat. Both the detox diet and the DASH diet use healthy foods with plenty of vegetables and fruits. Each recipe is guaranteed to be healthy and tasty. By using the Meal Finder book you will easily be able to plan your healthy meals for you and your whole family. And since this is a good combination of the two diet plans you have enough variety in which to choose you will not have to repeat too many meals in a couple weeks time.

You can do a couple of things to help make these diets work better for you. First thing is in planning. Since you have "found" your meals in the Meal Finder book you need to plan your grocery shopping trip accordingly. This starts with a good menu first. Write down the meals for a week or two or however long you need the menu. Once you have the menu planned you can then go through your kitchen and pantry and see what food you need to purchase in order to make the meals. Once you have an idea of what you have you can then create your grocery list. Write down all the food items you need and make a trip to the grocery store.

Once you get home with your groceries take some time to prep the food. This means to wash the fruits and vegetables. Chop the food that can be chopped and stored and just store the food that can't. Prepare as much as you can for your meals ahead of time to make it easier to cook the meals when the time comes. So many people don't want to do this because of all the preparation. If you do it in advance you will save yourself a ton of time and it won't feel as if you have to do too much.

Some of the recipes can even be completely prepared ahead of time. Perhaps you can get them together and store in the refrigerator for a final cook or heat through for later. Maybe you can cook and freeze some, so all you have to do is thaw and heat to have a nice home cooked meal. Look for ways to make your meal planning and preparing easier.

You are well on your way for dieting success. The planning stage sets the foundation. You planned well by getting this book and now have at your fingertips many good recipes that will help you to maintain a healthy lifestyle. In addition to the planning you can still do a few more things to help create a completely healthy lifestyle.

Drink plenty of water along with your meals. Water helps the body to stay hydrated. You should keep a glass or bottle of water with you at all times. You should sip on the water to keep from feeling too thirsty. Water is the perfect companion to both the detox and the DASH diet plans. Water will help to heal the body and is vital to good health.

Another healthy habit to develop and do in conjunction with a healthy diet is to exercise. The body needs regular exercise to keep it fit. Without exercise the body retains too much fat. Often when high blood pressure is diagnosed a physician may prescribe a change in diet along with moderate exercise. All you have to do is work out once every other day for at least half an hour to gain all the benefits from having a good exercise routine in your life.

Section 1: Detox Recipes

More than likely, you have heard about the detox diet, but you may not be familiar with all it entails or the benefits it has to offer. Maybe you like the idea of detoxifying your body, but you may not be sure where to begin or how to choose the right foods for easy detoxification. This ebook is packed with helpful information. Most of all, you'll find many excellent recipes that allow you to easily start cooking great meals that fit in with the detox diet. From great breakfast dishes to delicious desserts (yes you get to enjoy desserts on a detox diet), you'll find all kinds of great recipes and even a helpful meal plan guide to get you started.

Chapter 1: What is the Detox Diet?

Before you dive into learning how to cook foods that fit with the detox diet, it's important that you fully understand this diet. What is a detox diet? Basically, a detox diet is a diet that focuses on foods that help to remove toxins and excess waste from the body. While you will find many detox diets out there, these diets generally focus on the following:

- Increasing foods that offer antioxidants, nutrients and vitamins needed for natural detoxification
- Limits the chemicals that enter the body through food intake, done by eating organic and all natural foods
- Includes foods that include a lot of water and fiber, which help to eliminate more toxins by increasing urination and waste elimination through bowel movements

In most cases, a detox diet will encourage you to eat more vegetables and fruits, limiting other foods. Most diets also discourage eating processed foods. Alcohol is often eliminated and an increase in water consumption is encouraged as well.

Some people view detox diets as quite restrictive, since you are required to eliminate foods from your diet that may include toxins. For this reason, it's usually recommended that you only stay on a detox diet for a small time period for the best results.

Why do people decide to try a detox diet? Many people decide to give this diet a try because research has started suggesting that toxins that we ingest each day can be stored within fat cells in the body. Some people also eat diets that many lack important nutrients that aid in natural detoxification, which can lead to a buildup of toxins as well. Over time toxins may accumulate, leading to a variety of different problems. Most people want to eliminate these toxins, which is why they choose a detoxification diet.

It is important to note that many different detox diet plans are available. It's a good idea to check out different options, but if you are going on a detox diet for the first time, gentle plans will probably be your best option.

Chapter 2: Benefits of Detoxifying

If you're unsure whether you should give the detox diet a try, you'll definitely want to check out some of the excellent benefits of detoxifying the body. As you eat a diet that helps the body eliminate toxins, you'll notice a variety of benefits. The following are just a few of the top benefits you can enjoy when detoxifying the body with a good detox diet.

Benefit #1 – Lose Weight

Some people choose this diet simply because it offers the benefit of losing weight. Since you will no longer be taking in foods that include a high amount of fat and calories, you'll reduce the calories and fat you take in each day, which leads to weight loss. The high water and fiber intake encouraged on the detox diet will also help to eliminate excess waste from the body, which also aids with weight loss.

Benefit #2 – Improved Digestion

Since a detox diet focuses on eating nuts, fruits, grains,

seeds and veggies, you'll be ingesting more fiber than you did normally. As you increase fiber intake and water intake, it helps to cleanse the entire digestive system. You'll enjoy better digestion and avoid problems, like constipation.

Benefit #3 – Better Skin

Most people that follow a detox diet for a few days quickly begin noticing that their skin looks better. Toxins often affect the way your skin looks. Toxins can lead to blemishes and breakouts. As you eliminate more toxins, you'll notice an improvement in your overall skin tone.

Benefit #4 – Increased Energy

As toxins build up in the body, these toxins can affect your energy level, since the body is constantly battling toxins. After going on a detox diet, you may notice that your energy levels increase as your body begins eliminating the toxins that have caused fatigue. Within 5-7 days on a detox diet, most people report that their sleep better and they enjoy more energy than ever.

Of course, these are only a few of the benefits that can be enjoyed when you begin detoxifying the body. Some of the other benefits that you may enjoy include a reduction in your risk of heart disease, improved liver function, reduction in bloating and improved overall health.

Chapter 3: Helpful Tips for Detox Diet Success

If you're ready to go on a detox diet, it's a good idea to learn more about the diet, including some helpful tips for success. Diving right into the diet without planning ahead may lead to failure, which you definitely want to avoid. The following include preparation tips, information on what you should and shouldn't eat as well as information on the foods that offer the best detoxification punch.

Before You Go on a Detox Diet – Helpful Preparation Tips

Doing a bit of preparation can go a long way when you're ready to begin a detox diet. By following a few preparation tips, you can ensure you get the best cleansing results from your diet. Follow these helpful preparation tips to improve your results:

- Tip #1 – Start Weaning Off Caffeine – It's tough to quit caffeine cold turkey. If you are used to taking in caffeine, reduce withdrawal symptoms like headaches and fatigue by slowly weaning off caffeine. You may want to switch to decaf coffee or start drinking oolong, green or white tea.

- Tip #2 – Clean Out the Kitchen – You may find it tough to stick to your diet if you have processed foods, sweets, alcohol and other foods around that you should not be eating. Make sure these foods are out of the way before you go on the diet.

- Tip #3 – Begin Increasing Water Intake – Water intake is very important when you are on a detox diet. If you haven't been drinking enough water, start slowly increasing the amount of water you drink each day to build up to drinking what you'll need while detoxing.

- Tip #4 – Purchase Other Helpful Tools – Other tools can help increase your cleansing success, such as exfoliating brushes, that boost circulation and help eliminate toxins from the lymph system. Purchasing massage oils or essential oils for your bath can allow you to enjoy some relaxation as you adjust to the new diet.

What Should You Eat?

As you start the diet, it's a good idea to know what foods you should be including. Here is a list of some of the foods that you should be eating on a detox diet.

Vegetables:

- Broccoli sprouts
- Kale
- Swiss chard
- Kelp
- Broccoli
- Onions
- Beets
- Spinach
- Artichokes
- Garlic
- Cauliflower
- Collard greens
- Nori sheets

Fruits:

- Dried fruits
- Frozen fruits
- Fresh fruits
- Natural juices that are unsweetened

Seeds and Nuts:

- Walnuts
- Chia seeds
- Coconut
- Almonds
- Sunflower seeds
- Hemp seeds
- Natural nut butters
- Sesame seeds
- Pumpkin seeds
- Cashews

Starches and Grains:

- Buckwheat
- Wild rice
- Brown rice
- Amaranth
- Oats
- Millet
- Quinoa

Legumes and Beans:

- Green peas
- Adzuki beans
- Lentils
- Split yellow beans

Oils:

- Coconut oil
- Almond Oil
- Extra virgin olive oil
- Avocado oil
- Sunflower oil
- Hemp oil
- Chia oil
- Flax oil

Sweeteners:

- Stevia
- Raw honey
- Brown rice syrup
- Black strap molasses
- Real maple syrup

Drinks:

- Coconut milk (not canned)
- Green tea
- Unsweetened veggie and fruit juices
- Water
- Almond milk
- Hemp milk
- Rice milk
- Lemon water
- Herbal teas

What You Should NOT Eat

While there are plenty of foods you can eat, you should NOT be eating some foods while you are on a detox diet. Although diets can vary a bit, the following are some of the foods that are usually avoided by most detox diets.

Wheat Products:

Breads and pastas that contain wheat

Dairy Products:

- Cottage cheese
- Butter
- Frozen yogurt
- Ice cream
- Cheese
- Sour cream
- Milk

Sweeteners:

- Brown sugar
- Refined sugar
- High fructose corn syrup

- Artificial sweeteners
- Evaporated cane juice

Condiments:

- Soy sauce
- Mayonnaise
- Non-dairy creamers
- Relish
- Ketchup
- Steak sauce
- Teriyaki sauce

Animal Products:

- Pork
- Veal
- Beef
- Cold cuts
- Hot dogs
- sausages

Foods that Offer the Best Detoxification Punch

While we've already looked at some of the foods that are allowed on the detox diet, certain foods are power packed for better detoxification. The following are some of the foods that will offer you the best detoxification punch. Try adding more of these foods to your diet.

- Pomegranates – They are packed with antioxidants that help with detoxification. Some studies show that they help reduce inflammation, reduce aging and even help to reduce the risk of cancer.

- Garlic – Garlic has long been heralded for it's great health benefits and it includes certain compounds that can help fight off yeast and harmful bacteria within the digestive system, improving your ability to eliminate toxins. Garlic may also help to prevent certain cancers, diabetes and heart disease.

- Lemons – There's a reason you see lemons added to so many detox recipes. They have a lot of vitamin C in them and also can help to restore your body's alkaline to acid balance, which makes it easier for you to eliminate toxins from the body.

- Apples – Yes, apples offer great detoxification punch. Find ways to add more to your diet. They contain a high amount of insoluble fiber, which helps to eliminate waste and toxins from the digestive system.

- Quinoa – This is a great substitute for wheat products and it isn't a grain – it actually is a plant seed. It is packed with protein and includes lysine, which helps to repair the body's tissues.

- Almonds and Almond Products – Almonds allow you to enjoy milk while detoxing, since almond milk is easy to find. Almonds include a high amount of vitamin E, proteins, healthy fats, fiber and many other excellent nutrients that your body needs.

- Blueberries – You'll find that blueberries include plenty of vitamin C and a lot of fiber. They are one of the best fruits if you want to increase your intake of antioxidants that are important for eliminating toxins.

Chapter 4: Detox Diet Breakfast Recipes

Detox Friendly Buckwheat Pancakes

Even while you are working on a detox, you can still enjoy some delicious pancakes for breakfast. These delicious pancakes include chia seeds and buckwheat, which offer great fiber to help with your cleanse. Have fun adding toppings to these pancakes. Choose a bit of almond butter, a fruit topping or pure maple syrup.

What You'll Need:

½ cup of rice flour
¼ teaspoon of cinnamon
3 cups of water (add more or less to change to preferred consistency)
2 cups of buckwheat groats
¼ teaspoon of baking soda
Coconut oil
1 teaspoon of chia seeds
1 tablespoon of maple syrup

OPTIONAL: chopped apples, crushed nuts, carob chips,

berries

How to Make It:

In a blender or food processor, grind the buckwheat groats into flour. With a spice of coffee grinder, grind up the chia seeds until they become powdered. Combine the dry ingredients, then add the wet ingredients to the mix, stirring them until you have a smooth batter. Once you are done stirring, the batter should be very similar in consistency to traditional pancake batter.

Heat up a skillet on medium high heat. Add coconut oil to the skillet, allowing it to melt. Once oil is hot, pour in about ½ cup of batter and allow to spread, forming a pancake. Flip when bubbles begin to form on top.

Note: You can add more or less batter to the pan, depending on the size of the pancakes you want to make.

Vegetarian Breakfast Patty Recipe

These patties are vegetarian and while they don't have any meat in them, they offer plenty of great flavor. The mushrooms really add flavor to the patties and they are a perfect breakfast dish that works well with any detox diet. This recipe is inspired by a recipe featured on Epicurious.com from "The Great American Detox Diet."

What You'll Need:

1 tablespoon of wheat-free tamari
1 cup of rolled oats
1 cup of raw nuts, finely chopped
2 tablespoons of extra virgin olive oil
1 cup of cooked whole grains (i.e. brown rice)
2 tablespoons of spelt or brown rice flour
1 cup of minced button or shiitake mushrooms
1 ½ cups of play soy milk or vegetable stock, warm
½ cup of yellow onion, chopped
½ teaspoon of dried thyme
½ teaspoon of dried sage

How to Make It:

Heat a skillet on medium. Add tamari, flour and oil to the skillet, whisking quickly until well combined. Next, whisk in the milk or vegetable stock, allowing the mixture to cook until it begins to thicken, whisking continuously.

Remove mixture from the heat, then adding the nuts, mushrooms, oats, sage, rice, onion and thyme. Stir ingredients together until well combined, then placing mixture into a medium-sized mixing bowl. Allow the mixture to set for about 10 minutes at room temperature, then placing in the refrigerator for approximately 20 minutes or until it is cool enough for you to handle without burning yourself.

Preheat the oven to 350F.

Prepare a baking sheet, covering it with some parchment paper.

Take mixture out of the refrigerator, using a ¼ cup to scoop out some of the mix and make into a patty. Patties can be placed on the prepared baking sheet, allowing a small amount of space between patties.

Place patties in the oven, baking at 350 for 20 minutes. Serve hot. Patties can be frozen, but should be wrapped individually in some plastic wrap before placing them in an airtight container or freezer bag.

Easy Herbed Egg Omelet Recipe

Eggs are a great way to get some protein for breakfast when you are following a detox diet. This dish is ready in no time and can even be adapted to make a nice dinner as well. To get the perfect omelet, make sure you avoid overcooking it, allowing the top to be a bit on the soft side before the omelet is folded over.

What You'll Need:

2 tablespoons of fresh chives, chopped
3 green onions, chopped finely
5 eggs
1 tablespoon of fresh oregano, chopped
2 tablespoons of fresh coriander, chopped
2 tablespoons of fresh parsley, chopped
Salt and pepper to taste
Olive oil cooking spray

How to Make It:

In a medium bowl, whisk together two tablespoons of hot water and the eggs until they are well combined. Add the herbs, green onions, salt and pepper, mixing until combined.

Prepare an omelet pan with cooking spray, heating it up on medium heat. Once well heated, pour the eggs into the pan, cooking them for approximately five minutes or until the eggs have almost set. While the top is still a bit soft, fold the omelet. Cut it in half, serving it up while still hot.

Seedy Almond Spread Recipe

This delicious spread is a perfect topper for toast. It combines together delicious seeds and nuts, offering you plenty of protein, energy and a tasty breakfast option for your detox diet. If you don't want to use almonds, you can always use other types of nuts, such as hazelnuts, cashews, macadamias, pecans or pistachios to make the spread.

What You'll Need:

2/3 cup of pumpkin seeds
1/3 cup of sesame seeds
Sea salt to taste
2 ½ cups of almonds
Macadamia, canola or olive oil
2/3 cup of sunflower seeds

How to Make It:

Preheat the oven to 350F.

On a baking sheet, spread out the almonds evenly. Place them in the preheated oven, allowing them to roast for 4-5 minutes. Stir the nuts, then allow to roast for another 4-5 minutes or until the nuts are browned lightly.

On another baking sheet, spread out the sesame, pumpkin and sunflower seeds, allowing them to roast at 350 for about 5 minutes or until the pumpkin seeds have become browned lightly.

Allow the nuts and seeds to cool. Once cool, add seeds and nuts to a food processor, processing them until they are ground finely. A little at a time, add the oil of choice to the food processor through the top while the motor continues operating. Continue to add oil in small amounts until you have a thick paste. If desired, add a small amount of sea salt.

Place the spread in an air tight container, storing in the refrigerator for up to two months.

Apple Nut Oatmeal Recipe

Oatmeal is a great breakfast choice when you're on a detox diet. It offer plenty of great fiber, helps to keep blood sugar stabilized and the addition of nuts helps give you some extra energy. The apple provides some sweetness to the meal. It's easy to make and you can vary the nuts and fruits to make this recipe to your own unique tastes.

What You'll Need:

3 cups of water
½ cup of apple, diced
½ teaspoon of cinnamon
1 cup of steel-cut or rolled oats
½ cup of ground walnuts (you can substitute in pecans or almonds too)
1 teaspoon of vanilla
¼ cup of ground flax seed
Honey or maple syrup to taste
Pinch of salt

How to Make It:

In a large saucepan, bring the sea salt and water to a boil. Once it reaches a boil, reduce the heat, adding the oats to the water. Allow to cook according to package directions, stirring from time to time. In the last five minutes of cooking, add the vanilla, cinnamon and apples to the saucepan.

When oats are done cooking, turn off the heat, then stirring in the nuts and flax seeds. Cover the oats and allow to sit for 3-5 minutes. Add syrup or honey to taste and then serve hot with almond milk. You can also top the oatmeal off with more fresh fruit if you desire. Makes two servings.

Homemade Apple Cinnamon Granola Recipe

While you're on a detox diet, it's probably best to avoid boxed granola, since it probably contains refined sugars and refined grain products. However, it's pretty easy to make your own delicious granola, which makes a tasty breakfast you can enjoy any morning. You are in control of the ingredients you place in this granola, which means you can pack it with wholesome ingredients that work with your diet. Follow this recipe and then have fun making your own substitutions to create your own variations of this granola recipe.

What You'll Need:

½ cup of almonds, chopped
2 ½ cups of rolled oats
1 tart apple, diced
½ cup of amaranth flour
2 teaspoons of cinnamon
½ cup of coconut, safflower or sunflower oil
½ cup of raisins
½ cup of maple syrup
½ cup of pumpkin seeds
½ teaspoon of nutmeg

How to Make It:

Preheat the oven to 350F.

In a large mixing bowl, mix together all the dry ingredients. Add the wet ingredients to the bowl, stirring everything together until everything is well combined and moistened.

On two baking sheets sprayed with cooking spray, spread out the granola mixture in an even layer. Place in the oven, baking at 350 for about 25-30 minutes or until the mixture is a nice, golden brown. After 15 minutes in the oven, use a spatula to flip or stir the granola.

Remove granola from the oven, allowing to cool completely. Store granola in an airtight container. Makes about 10 cups of granola.

Variation Ideas:

- Fruits: blueberries, pears, dates, cranberries, cherries, figs
- Spices: cardamom, nutmeg, ginger
- Nuts: walnuts, cashews, macadamia, pecans, brazil
- Seeds: hemp, sesame, sunflower, chia, flax

Date Porridge Recipe

Since dates have plenty of great nutrients and fiber, they are a great addition to your detox diet. They also provide some natural sweetness to this porridge, which means you don't need to add other sweeteners. Add other nuts and fruits as toppings to make this recipe even more interesting for your taste buds.

What You'll Need:

2 cups of rolled oats
½ cup of pistachio nuts, shelled and chopped roughly
2 cups of fresh dates
Pinch of salt
2 cups of non-dairy milk
2 cups of water

How to Make It:

Start by making a puree from your dates. Cut the dates in half, removing the stems and pits. In a large saucepan, bring some water to a boil. Remove from heat, adding dates to the water. Cover and allow dates to soak for about 30 minutes or until they are soft. Strain away all but six tablespoons of the water.

Take off the dates' skin, adding them to a food processor. Add the reserved water to the processor, processing until you have a nice puree.

In a saucepan, bring the milk, 2 cups of water and the salt to a boil. Add oats, allowing to boil and then reducing heat until the oats are simmering. Allow to simmer for about 5 minutes or until the oats are well cooked. Stir regularly while cooking.

Add oats to a bowl. Cover with some of the date puree, topping with some of the chopped nuts. Add any other nuts or fruit you may want to add to the porridge. If you feel it needs extra sweetener, add maple syrup or honey.

Chapter 5: Detox Diet Soup and Salad Recipes

Detox Minestrone Soup Recipe

This Minestrone soup offers a nice combination of high fiber beans and delicious vegetables, which makes it a perfect soup to eat while you're on a detox diet. You'll get plenty of protein from the beans and a good dose of nutrients from all the veggies included. Serve the soup alone or serve up it with a whole grain for a full meal.

What You'll Need:

3 cloves of garlic, minced
1 large onion, chopped
2-3 carrots, peeled and chopped
2 celery stalks, chopped
1 can of garbanzo beans (15 oz.)
1 can of crushed or diced tomatoes (15 oz.)
1 can of kidney beans (15 oz.)
Italian spices to taste (oregano, marjoram, basil, thyme, rosemary)
Pepper and salt to taste

Olive Oil

How to Make It:

Add a small amount of olive oil to a large pot and heat on medium heat. Add garlic and onion, sautéing until the onion is tender and transparent. Add in the spices and celery, allowing to sauté for about 5 more minutes. Next, add in the beans, tomatoes and carrots. Cover all ingredients with water. Bring the mixture to a boil. Once boiling, reduce the heat, allowing the soup to simmer for 20-30 minutes. Season with pepper and salt to taste. Serve hot. Makes four servings.

Gazpacho Soup Recipe

Full of tomatoes, you'll get great nutrients from this soup. The addition of other vegetables makes it a delicious way to stick to your detox diet. This soup is wonderful for summer, since it's cool.

What You'll Need:

½ medium cucumber, chopped
1 shallot, chopped
1 bell pepper of any color, chopped
2 tablespoons of extra virgin olive oil
3-4 large tomatoes
1 clove of garlic, chopped
½ tablespoon of chili flakes
2 limes, rind removed
½ bunch of cilantro
1 tablespoon of apple cider vinegar
1 cup of ice water
Pepper and salt to taste

How to Make It:

Wash tomatoes, coring them and then quickly dropping into boiling water to blanch for about a minute. Remove tomatoes from boiling water, placing them immediately in iced water, which will make the skins easy to remove. Remove the skins and then dice up tomatoes. Place the tomatoes in a food processor.

Set 1/3 of the cucumber and peppers to the side for later. Add everything else into the food processor with the tomatoes. Process until the mixture is smooth. Remove soup from the processor, adding the rest of the cucumber and peppers to the soup, stirring to incorporate. Serve. Makes two servings.

Delicious Lemon Dressed Kale Salad Recipe

This kale salad is packed with great vegetables that will help your detox. The addition of the lemon dressing adds a nice pop of flavor that compliments the kale and other vegetables included. When making this recipe, go with curly-leafed kale, which will look great in the salad.

What You'll Need:

Salad:

1 carrot, peeled and grated
1 avocado, peeled and sliced
2 tablespoons of extra virgin olive oil
2 scallions, minced
¼ teaspoon of sea salt
1 bunch of kale
1 teaspoon of sunflower seeds (raw preferred)
1 beet, sliced

Dressing:

1 tablespoon of extra virgin olive oil
Dash of sea salt
Juice from one lemon, plus the zest
Ground fresh pepper

1 teaspoon of agave nectar (or substitute with honey)

How to Make It:

In a large salad bowl, toss together the kale, ¼ teaspoon of the salt and the olive oil. Use hands to massage salt and oil into the kale for several minutes. Place kale in the refrigerator, allowing to sit for 5-7 minutes.

Remove kale from refrigerator. Add beet, sunflower seeds, carrot, scallions and avocado to the bowl. Toss gently.

In a measuring cup of dressing bottle, mix together the dressing ingredients. Ensure ingredients are mixed well. Pour dressing over the salad. Serve immediately.

Tuscan Veggie Bean Soup Recipe

Cannellini beans add fiber and protein to this soup and plenty of vegetables add great nutrients to the delicious soup. Experiment with adding different vegetables to vary the flavor a bit. Prepare the beans the night before to make sure this recipe comes together quickly the next day.

What You'll Need:

1 tablespoon of olive oil
4 cloves of garlic, chopped
2 Desiree potatoes, peeled and diced into one inch pieces
½ cup of dried cannellini beans (soaked in cold water overnight)
8 cups of vegetable stock
1 cup of green beans, snapped and trimmed
2 carrots, peeled and then chopped
1 onion, thinly sliced
6 Roma tomatoes, peeled, seeded and diced
1 celery stalk, chopped

How to Make It:

Drain cannellini beans, then cover them with water and

allow to simmer for approximately 30 minutes or until the beans become tender. Drain the beans.

In a large saucepan, heat up the olive oil, adding onion and cooking until it becomes soft and transparent. Add the celery, stock, potatoes, carrots, tomatoes, carrots and garlic to the pan. Add seasonings to taste, then allow the soup to simmer uncovered until the vegetables become tender, about 35-40 minutes.

Add the cooked cannellini beans to the soup and then stir in the green beans. Allow the soup to continue simmering for about 15-20 minutes. Serve while hot. Makes about 6-8 servings.

Grapefruit and Sesame Salad Recipe

The flavors of this delightful salad will definitely stimulate your taste buds while making sure you get plenty of greens and the benefits of delicious grapefruit. Grapefruit is wonderful for helping to detox the body. Enjoy the salad for lunch or curb cravings by having it for a nice afternoon snack.

What You'll Need:

2 large handfuls of baby spring greens
3 tablespoons of walnuts or almonds
¼ cup of sesame tahini
2 tablespoons of honey
1 grapefruit

How to Make It:

Wash the greens before using, then placing them in a medium salad bowl. Remove the skin from the grapefruit, cutting up the flesh into pieces that are bite-sized. Add the grapefruit pieces to the greens.

Mix together the honey and tahini, then pour the dressing over the salad. Top with the nuts, serving immediately. Makes two servings.

Miso Soup Recipe

This soup has been made and consumed in Japan for hundreds of years. The Japanese eat it to help with digestion, which makes it a wonderful dish to add to your detox diet. You'll also find that the soup is packed with minerals, vitamins and plenty of protein. For the best soup, it's best to avoid adding the miso until you are almost ready to serve the soup. The miso should never be boiled.

What You'll Need:

2 stalks of celery, finely chopped
1 clove of garlic, finely chopped
4 cups of water
½ inch of fresh ginger root, finely chopped
1 carrot, finely chopped
Tamari to taste
2-4 tablespoons of the miso paste (depending on the strength and taste you want to achieve)

How to Make It:

Place chopped vegetables in a medium sauce pan. In another tea pot or pan, heat up the four cups of water until it is boiling. Pour the boiling water over vegetables in the sauce pan, allowing them to steep for several minutes. Allow to cool enough that you can easily place your finger in the mixture for a few seconds.

Remove a couple scoops of the liquid and place in a small bowl. Next, add miso paste to the liquid, mixing until the mixture is completely smooth. Make sure there are no lumps. Place this mixture back into the soup, stirring to incorporate completely. Add a bit of extra flavor with some tamari to taste. Serve immediately.

Note: You can increase the nutrients in the soup by adding more vegetables. To provide a heartier meal, the soup can be served over cooked whole grains or rice noodles.

Cleansing Seaweed Salad Recipe

Seaweed is an excellent addition to your diet, since it helps to eliminate toxins, can help to reduce blood pressure and offers plenty of great vitamins and minerals as well. If you have a hard time finding the seaweed called for in the recipe, check in a whole foods store, an Asian market or check out the Asian area of a grocery store in your area.

What You'll Need:

1 tablespoon of dried arame, crushed
2-4 romaine lettuce leaves
½ teaspoon of sesame seeds
2 teaspoons of dried wakame, crushed
Pinch of red chili paste or flakes
1 teaspoon of toasted sesame oil
¼ teaspoon of ume plum vinegar

How to Make It:

In a saucepan, heat up two cups of water until it comes to a boil. Remove the water from the heat, adding in the wakame and arame. Allow the seaweed to sit for about 10 minutes or until you have soft, hydrated seaweed.

Chop up the romaine leaves into 1-2 inch pieces, placing pieces in two serving bowls.

Strain the water from the seaweed, squeezing out any extra moisture from the seaweed. Place the seaweed in a medium mixing bowl, then add the oil, red chili, vinegar and sesame seeds to the bowl, stirring up until the ingredients are combined.

Serve the seaweed mixture on top of the romaine lettuce. Makes two servings.

Easy Black Bean Chili Recipe

Black beans add great fiber and protein to this chili and the addition of some turkey breast adds even more filling protein. This soup is hearty enough to eat for dinner.

What You'll Need:

½ cup of chopped onion
1 8-oz pack of seasoned rice and black beans
1 can of diced tomatoes (14.5 oz.)
2 teaspoons of extra virgin olive oil
¼ cup of scallions, chopped
1 teaspoon of chili powder
½ pound of ground turkey
½ cup of chopped onion
½ teaspoon of ground cumin

How to Make It:

In a large saucepan, heat the olive oil on medium high heat. Place onion in the heated oil, sautéing it for about 2-3 minutes. Next, place turkey in the pan, allowing it to brown, which should take 2-5 minutes. Make sure you break up the turkey as it is cooking. Add chili powder, rice and beans and cumin to the pan. Add the water called for on the package. Place tomatoes in the mix, then heat until the soup comes to a boil. Once boiling, reduce the heat, simmering on low until the liquid has been absorbed by the rice and the rice is the desired tenderness. Stir from time to time while cooking. Serve in bowls, topping with the chopped scallions. Makes six servings.

Chapter 6: Side Dish Detox Recipes

Tasty Roasted Roots Recipe

Root vegetables offer a nourishing side dish that will help fill you up while you're on the detox diet. They offer complex carbs, which can help keep your blood sugar stable while helping to minimize cravings for sweets as well. The great root veggies used in this recipe will help cleanse your body and they taste amazing too. Have fun trying out different veggie combinations and experiment with different spices to add plenty of flavor as well.

What You'll Need:

4 medium red potatoes, quartered
2-3 large carrots, cut into large chunks
1 large onion, cut into large pieces
1-2 leeks, cut into chunks
2-3 Daikon radishes, chunked
Olive oil
Basil and oregano to taste
Pepper and salt to taste

How to Make It:

Preheat the oven to 375F.

Chop up all the veggies into chunks. Make sure the chunks are as uniform as possible for even cooking. Place veggies in a large bowl. Drizzle with some olive oil and then sprinkle in basil, oregano, pepper and salt. Toss the vegetables to coat them with the oil and spices.

Place veggies in a large baking dish that has been prepared with non-stick cooking spray. Bake at 375 for 45-60 minutes, making sure vegetables are browned and tender. Toss halfway through cooking.

Mix and Match These Root Veggies: Winter squash, turnips, onions, yams, beets, radish, carrots, garlic, parsnips, leeks

Mix and Match Different Spices: curry, cumin, garlic powder, parsley, thyme, rosemary, Chinese 5 spice, garam masala, sage, oregano, basil, Old Bay

Burdock Carrot Stir Fry Recipe

The addition of burdock to this recipe adds some excellent detox benefits to the dish, since it is known to help support liver function, eliminate uric acid and promotes kidney function as well. This recipe combines together some great root veggies for plenty of flavor. Makes a great side dish that goes well with many meals.

What You'll Need:

14 inches of burdock root, fresh
1 cup of cilantro, chopped
Toasted sesame seed oil
1 inch of ginger root, fresh
4 medium to large carrots
½ a lemon juice with ¼ cup of purified water added to it
Sea salt
Purified water

How to Make It:

Peel the ginger, then mince it up into fine pieces. Next, wash the carrots and burdock, allowing the skin to stay. Slice carrots and burdock into thin slices. Chop up the cilantro.

Place a large skillet on medium heat, covering its bottom with some purified water, using just enough to ensure the bottom is covered. Add the carrot, burdock and ginger to the water. Allow to sauté in the water for 5-6 minutes on medium high. Add the lemon juice combined with ¼ of water, as well as the cilantro to the mix. Cover the skillet, allowing the ingredients to steam for another 5-6 minutes.

Drizzle the vegetables with some toasted sesame oil to taste, sprinkling with the desired amount of seal salt. Serve alone while hot or serve up over quinoa or brown rice. Makes two servings.

Easy Spinach and Cabbage Pie Recipe

This recipe is packed with spinach, which offers many beneficial vitamins and nutrients. All the great spices make sure that this pie is full of flavor. This is hearty enough to serve alone, but it also makes a great side dish for any meal.

What You'll Need:

¾ teaspoon of sea salt, divided
½ cup of onion, chopped
½ cup of zucchini, chopped
2 cups of spelt white flour
8 cups of baby spinach, fresh, washed and well dried
1/3 cup of extra virgin olive oil, plus an extra tablespoon
1 clove of garlic, minced
¼ teaspoon of ground red pepper
½ teaspoon of dried marjoram
1-2 tablespoons of water
½ cup of red cabbage, finely shredded
½ teaspoon of dried thyme
1 teaspoon of paprika
1 large tomato, cut up into 8 slices (half-moon in shape)
1 teaspoon of dried mustard powder
½ teaspoon of dried basil

How to Make It:

Preheat the oven to 375F.

Start preparing the pie crust by sifting together a ¼ teaspoon of the sea salt with the flour. Place into a medium-sized mixing bowl. While stirring continuously, slowly add 1/3 cup of the olive oil, working to form a nice dough. Avoid over mixing the dough or you'll end up with tough dough. Use the 1-2 tablespoons of water to help create the pie dough.

Work dough into a ball, using a rolling pin to roll it out lightly into a 9-inch circle. Once dough is rolled out, place dough in a prepared 9-inch pie plate, pressing it into the pan securely. Use a fork to poke several places on the bottom of the crust to keep it from bubbling up in the oven. Set to the side and work on the filling.

Heat up the rest of the olive oil in a medium skillet on medium. Add the onion to the hot oil, allowing to sauté for about 2-3 minutes. Add the zucchini and cabbage, allowing the veggies to sauté for another 5-6 minutes. Place spinach in the pan with the veggies, sautéing only until the spinach has started to wilt. Add the basil, paprika, pepper, marjoram, garlic, salt, mustard and thyme to the pan, stirring everything together and allowing to sauté for one more minute.

Pour the vegetable mixture into the pie crust. Place pie in the oven, baking at 375 for 35 minutes. When pie is done, remove from the oven, garnishing it with the tomato slices. Serve while still warm. Makes 4-6 servings.

Chapter 7: Main Dish Detox Diet Recipes

Vegetarian Black Bean Burgers Recipe

There's no need to live without your favorite burgers when you are on a detox diet. In fact, you can go with a delicious vegetarian burger that provides plenty of protein and great fiber to help you with your detox. Top these burgers with tomatoes and lettuce and you'll have a tasty dinner that will leave you feeling satisfied. You can even make a double batch of the recipe, freezing the extras for a later time when you need a quick meal.

What You'll Need:

1 clove of garlic
2 cups of quinoa
1 teaspoon of red pepper flakes, mild
2 carrots
3 cups of black beans, cooked (you can substitute in kidney beans if you want)
1 tablespoon of olive oil
¼ cup of purified water
2 teaspoons of cumin

½ red onion
¼ cup of lemon juice
1 teaspoon of coriander
1 head of bok choy, small
½ cup of arrowroot powder
1 tablespoon of safflower oil
1 teaspoon of sea salt

How to Make It:

Cook the quinoa according to the instructions on the package, setting to the site.

Meanwhile, mince the onions and garlic, chop up the bok choy and peel and grate the carrots.

In a skillet, heat olive oil over medium heat. Add the veggies, along with the cumin, red pepper and the coriander to the skillet. Sauté the vegetables until they are tender.

In a food processor or blender, process the salt, water, black beans, lemon juice and arrowroot powder until you have a smooth mixture.

In a large mixing bowl, combine the sautéed veggies, the cooked quinoa and the bean mixture. Mix until well combined. Place mixture in the refrigerator, allowing to chill for a minimum of 2 hours.

After chilling, add safflower oil to a skillet, preheating it on medium high heat. Once the oil is hot, create patties from the mixture. Patties should be about ¼ inch thick. Fry up the patties in the oil, cooking each side for about five minutes, ensuring the patties are well browned. Serve up patties with or without bread, topping with desired veggies. Makes 4-6 servings.

Red Snapper and Kale Recipe

Fish is a wonderful food to add to your detox diet. It's low in calories but offers plenty of stomach filling protein. With the addition of peppercorns, red peppers, basil and lemon, this recipe will make your taste buds sing. It's definitely proof that you don't have to rely on bland, tasteless foods while following the detox diet.

What You'll Need:

1 teaspoon of peppercorns
1 cup of fresh basil
1 bay leaf
2 pounds of kale
3 tablespoons of extra virgin olive oil
1 lemon, juiced
2 red peppers
2 teaspoons of garlic, minced
6 pieces of red snapper, 4 ounces each

How to Make It:

Preheat the oven to 300F.

In a shallow baking dish, add the pieces of snapper, covering them with water. Add bay leaf, peppercorns and the lemon juice to the water. Place the baking dish with snapper into the oven, allowing to cook for 30 minutes or until the fish is completely cooked through.

Meanwhile, add olive oil to a skillet, heating over medium heat. Add garlic and kale, sautéing for several minutes. Once kale is done sautéing, place it on a plate. Take peppers, broiling them until they are blackened or place them on a gas burner, allowing them to blacken. Remove the seeds and the skin, then dice up the roasted peppers. In the skillet, heat up olive oil and then sauté the basil and peppers together. Place to the side, allowing the peppers and basil to cool. Once cool, place in a blender or food processor, pureeing it into a smooth mixture.

Before serving, divide up the sautéed kale, placing some on six different dinner plates. Remove cooked fish from the baking dish, placing a piece of fish on top of each mound of kale. Top with the pepper basil mixture. Serve while warm. Makes six servings.

Tasty Green Leaf Lettuce Wraps Recipe

Lettuce is a low calorie way to wrap up a tasty main dish without using bread. It adds plenty of crunch and creates a beautiful dish as well. These green leaf lettuce wraps look great and are filled with delicious ingredients that make a wonderful main dish that can be served up any time. Save a couple to take with you to work for lunch the next day.

What You'll Need:

1 cup of carrots, grated
½ cucumber, seeded and sliced into slices about ¼ thick
1 cup of guacamole
1 cooked fillet of salmon or a cooked chicken breast, cooked and then shredded or flaked
8 large green leaf lettuce leaves
1 cup of broccoli or alfalfa sprouts

How to Make It:

Wash lettuce leaves, then allow leaves to dry. Cut off about an inch of the stem on the bottom of lettuce leaves. Place leaves on a clean surface.

Add about two tablespoons of the guacamole to each

lettuce leaf, spreading it carefully across the leaf. Next, sprinkle in two tablespoons of sprouts, two tablespoons of cucumbers and two tablespoons of the carrots.

Lay 2-3 tablespoons of shredded salmon or chicken on top of the veggies. Then, roll up the lettuce leaves, starting on one side until you have a completed wrap. Eat immediately. Makes four servings.

Salmon Fillets with Orange Glaze Recipe

Once you take a single bite of this delicious salmon recipe, you'll be hooked. The amazing orange glaze adds a bit of zing to the fish. It's easy to make and will be done in no time at all, for a quick, easy dinner. Serve up with some steamed veggies and you may even want to add a cooked whole grain on the side as well.

What You'll Need:

2 teaspoons of sesame oil
1 tablespoon of cornstarch
½ cup of orange juice
2 tablespoons of soy sauce
1 tablespoon of filtered water
1 tablespoon of fresh ginger, grated
4 4-oz salmon fillets

How to Make It:

Combine the sesame oil, orange juice, soy sauce and ginger together in a medium sized bowl. Add the fillets of salmon to the bowl, covering the fillets and placing in the refrigerator for 30-40 minutes.

Preheat the broiler.

Remove the fish from the refrigerator, draining the fish but keeping the marinade for later. Prepare a broiler pan by lining it with foil and then oiling it or spraying with non-stick spray. Place the fillets on the pan, placing in the oven under the broiler. Allow to broil for 10-15 minutes, making sure the fish is fully cooked.

Meanwhile, place the reserved marinade in a small saucepan. Bring it to a boil. In a small measuring cup, mix together the water and cornstarch until well combined. Add the cornstarch slurry to the boiling marinade, allowing to cook for a minute, ensuring that the sauce begins to thicken. Remove from the heat.

Place salmon on four dinner plates, serving with the orange glaze on the side for dipping. Makes four servings.

Wild Rice and Chicken Recipe

It's nice to have some recipes that you can quickly prepare while on the detox diet and this recipe is easy and fast, making it perfect for busy weeknights. The delicious wild rice tastes wonderful with the chicken and it's easy to make because you're using a boxed wild rice mix. The addition of broccoli adds a wonderful vegetable to the dish, providing a well-rounded meal in a single dish.

What You'll Need:

1 teaspoon of dried thyme
2 tablespoons of fresh parsley, chopped
1 teaspoon of extra virgin olive oil
1 cup of cooked chicken, cubed
2 cups of fresh broccoli florets (or you can use frozen broccoli that has been thawed)
4.5 ounce box of wild rice and brown rice combined with mushrooms (or other similar wild rice mix)

How to Make It:

Cook up the wild rice, following the instructions on the package. Use the seasoning packet to season to your own taste, adding the thyme and olive oil to the rice while cooking.

While the rice cooks, steam the broccoli. Once the broccoli is cooked, reserve until rice is almost done cooking. About a minute or two before the rice is done cooking, add the broccoli to the rice. When rice has finished cooking, toss the mixture with the chopped parsley and the chicken. Serve while hot. Makes four servings.

Scallop and Leek Risotto Recipe

Scallops offer a delicious way to get plenty of protein while still sticking to your detox diet. You'll get plenty of flavor with these scallops, since the recipe includes dill, garlic, fennel and leeks. Enjoy with tender, cooked Arborio rice for a full meal that will satisfy your stomach and your taste buds.

What You'll Need:

1 large fennel bulb, cored and trimmed, then chopped finely
1 ½ cups of Arborio rice
Olive oil
1 clove of garlic, chopped
1 leek, only the white parts, chopped
1 tablespoon of fresh dill, chopped
4 cups of chicken or fish stock
2 teaspoons of butter
20 large scallops, no roe

How to Make It:

In a large-size saucepan, heat up a tablespoon of olive oil. Add fennel and leek, covering and cooking over low heat until leek and fennel are soft. If veggies begin sticking, add a small amount of stock to the pan. Add the rice and garlic to the saucepan, stirring while cooking on medium heat. Cook until the rice is coated in oil and lightly toasted. Meanwhile, simmer stock in another large saucepan.

Add a cup of the stock to the pan containing the rice, stirring it in until the stock has been absorbed. Add the rest of the stock about a half cup at a time, continuing to stir and allowing each bit of stock to be well absorbed before you add more to the pan. After adding all the stock, add 2/3 of the dill and the butter to the pan, adding salt and pepper to taste.

Remove the pan from the heat, covering and then allowing to stand for 5-7 minutes.

While rice is standing, brush the scallops lightly with a bit of olive oil, chargrilling them on each side until they are cooked. Place scallops on a plate.

Place risotto in bowls, topping them with scallops and the juices from the scallops. Top with the leftover dill. Makes 4 servings.

Lemon Rosemary Chicken Recipe

The delicious flavors of lemon and rosemary make this chicken something special. This chicken is wonderful served up with steamed veggies, wild rice pilaf and a side salad.

What You'll Need:

1 whole chicken, cut into pieces
2 lemons, sliced
½ cup of green olives, sliced
2 cloves of garlic, chopped
2 tablespoons of extra virgin olive oil
1 medium onion, chopped
½ cup of black olives, sliced
3 sprigs of fresh rosemary
1 tablespoons of rinsed capers

How to Make It:

In a skillet or sauté pan, heat up the olive oil over medium heat. Add chicken to the pan, cooking for about 10-12 minutes or until well browned. Remove chicken from the pan, setting to the side. Eliminate any extra fat, leaving just a little film of olive oil and fat in the bottom of the pan.

Add onion to the pan, cooking for 2-3 minutes on medium heat. Place garlic in the pan with the onion, allowing to cook for a minute or two. Place chicken back in the pan, then add the olives, capers, lemon and rosemary. Cover the pan, allowing the chicken to cook for another 25-30 minutes, or until the chicken is completely cooked. Baste the chicken from time to time. Serve hot. Makes four servings.

Easy Stir Fried Veggies and Fish Recipe

Fish is an excellent protein choice to eat while on a detox diet and this recipe is packed with excellent veggies as well, which helps detox your body. Delicious orange roughy is the fish of choice and this recipe allows you to make an entire dinner in a reasonably short amount of time.

What You'll Need:

1 clove of garlic, minced
1 cup of celery, sliced
1 ½ tablespoons of extra virgin olive oil
½ cup of orange juice
1 teaspoon of rice vinegar
1 shallot, minced
1 teaspoon of soy sauce
1 cup of water chestnuts, sliced
1 cup of red pepper, chopped
1 teaspoon of sesame oil
1 cup of fresh, trimmed snow peas
2 teaspoons of cornstarch
2 cups of brown rice, cooked
1 ½ pounds of orange roughy, cut into 1.5 inch pieces and skin removed

How to Make It:

In a large, heavy skillet, heat up a tablespoon of the olive oil on medium high. Once oil is hot, add the pieces of fish, stir frying until the fish is fully cooked. Remove fish and place on a plate to the side.

Add the rest of the olive oil to the skillet, allowing it to get hot. Then, add the shallot and garlic, allowing it to stir fry for about a minute. Place water chestnuts, show peas, red pepper and celery in the pan, covering and allowing the vegetables to steam for 2-3 minutes.

Meanwhile, combined together the cornstarch, rice vinegar, sesame oil, soy sauce and orange juice in a small bowl or a measuring cup. Once combined, add to the skillet with the veggies, allowing it to cook until thicken, which should take about a minute. Add fish back to the skillet, allowing it to cook for another couple of minutes or until warmed through.

Serve stir fried fish and veggies over hot brown rice, topping with chopped green onions. Makes four servings.

Lemon Ginger Braised Shrimp Recipe

Lemon and ginger, along with some other seasonings, add big flavor to this delicious shrimp dish. Shrimp is an excellent protein choice for your detox diet, since it is low calorie, low in fat and packs a huge protein punch. The asparagus adds plenty of great nutrients to the meal, as do the carrots.

What You'll Need:

1 cup of celery, chopped
1 lemon, juiced
1 cup of carrots, chopped
1/3 teaspoon of cloves
2 teaspoons of extra virgin olive oil
¼ cup of Bragg Liquid Aminos
3 tablespoons of ginger, minced
1 large onion, chunked
3 cloves of garlic, minced
2 sprigs of parsley, minced
2 cups of vegetable stock or filtered water
1 pound of asparagus, cleaned and trimmed
1 pound of cleaned and peeled large shrimp

How to Make It:

Combine the lemon juice and Bragg Aminos together, pressing and grinding 2 of the minced garlic cloves into the mixture. Place shrimp in a plastic ziplock bag, adding the lemon juice mixture and allowing the shrimp to marinate for a couple hours in the refrigerator.

In a large pot, heat up the olive oil on medium, adding the celery, onion and the last clove of garlic. Allow veggies to sauté until they begin browning, which should take 2-3 minutes. Next, add in the cloves, 2 tablespoons of the minced ginger, parsley, water (or stock) and the carrots.

Bring the vegetables and liquid to a boil. Add shrimp and asparagus to a steamer basket, sprinkling with the rest of the ginger. Place the steamer basket in the large pot with the rest of the ingredients. Cover the pot, allowing the shrimp and asparagus to steam until the shrimp is fully cooked – about 5-6 minutes.

Place steamed asparagus on a plate, topping it with the shrimp. Ladle the broth and veggies over each serving of shrimp and asparagus. Top with some freshly chopped parsley. Makes four servings.

Chapter 8: Detox Drink and Detox Smoothie Recipes

Delicious Strawberry Smoothie Recipe

Strawberries offer an excellent way to get vitamin C, which helps give your immune system a boost. This recipe adds tofu to the smoothie, which adds some calcium and a lot of protein. While you may be leery of adding tofu to a smoothie, it blends right in and you will not notice it with the wonderful flavor of the other smoothie ingredients.

What You'll Need:

½ cup of silken tofu
2 tablespoons of clear honey
1 lemon, juiced
1 ¾ cups of strawberries
2 large oranges, juiced
3 tablespoons of sunflower or pumpkin seeds

How to Make It:

Chop up the tofu into rough pieces. Next, hull

strawberries and then chop or slice them. Keep a few slices or chunks back to add as a garnish when the smoothie is finished.

Place the orange juice, lemon juice, honey, tofu, strawberries and seeds in the blender or use a food processor. Blend together until you have a creamy, smooth mixture. Scrape down from time to time if needed. Pour into large glasses and enjoy right away. Makes two servings.

Delicious Green Cleansing Juice Recipe

Green veggies contain chlorophyll and that chlorophyll is thought to help with detoxification. This delicious juice has plenty of chlorophyll in it. Most people enjoy drinking this juice, since it is so refreshing and light. You will feel like you're cleansing yourself from the inside out. To add to its refreshing quality, add some ice to the juice.

What You'll Need:

½ green capsicum, seeded
2 granny smith apples, cored and quartered
2 green cucumbers
6 sprigs of fresh parsley, with the stems

How to Make It:

Cut up the apples and the veggies into small enough chunks to fit into your juice extractor's feed tube. Begin processing the apples, parsley and veggies. Pour the juice into a pitcher or jug, making sure you mix it up well. Drink the juice right away, adding some ice to chill it if you want. Makes two servings.

Tropical Pineapple Smoothie

This smoothie brings together the delicious flavors of oranges, bananas and pineapple, providing an intense tropical taste. The romaine in the mix is surprising and adds plenty of greens to the smoothie, packing in more nutrients. This one is easy to make and is great for breakfast or even a nice snack later in the day.

What You'll Need:

2 bananas
½ head of romaine lettuce
¼ of a fresh pineapple
1 orange
2 cups of water

How to Make It:

Peel the orange and the bananas. Chop orange and bananas into chunks. Chop up the pineapple into chunks as well. Take the romaine lettuce and chop it up roughly. In a blender, combine the bananas, romaine lettuce, pineapple, orange and water together. Blend until smooth. Serve right away. Makes 2 servings.

Cacao Powder Smoothie Recipe

If you want to enjoy some chocolate flavor in your smoothie, adding in some raw cacao powder is an excellent idea. Just remember, it can be quite stimulating, so you may not want to have this smoothie late in the evening before you go to bed. Instead of grabbing for chocolate, try this smoothie, which allows you to stick to your detox diet while enjoying the delicious chocolate flavor.

What You'll Need:

2 large handfuls of spinach leaves
1 pear
1 apple
½ head of romaine lettuce
1 teaspoon of green powder (like Spirulina)
2 bananas
2 cups of water
1-2 tablespoons of raw cacao powder

How to Make It:

Chop the spinach and romaine lettuce up roughly. Peel pear, apple and bananas, then cut up the fruit into chunks. Add the spinach, pear, apple, romaine, green powder, bananas, water and cacao powder to a blender or a food processor. Begin blending until ingredients are well blended and smooth. Serve right away. Makes 2 servings.

Tasty Berry Juice Recipe

Blueberries, which are used in this juice recipe, are full of vitamins, antioxidants and great antibacterial compounds. The addition of red grapes and blackberries adds even more nutrition to this juice recipe. The combination of berries makes a delicious juice that you are sure to enjoy. Makes a great addition to any breakfast.

What You'll Need:

1 cup of blueberries
1 cup of blackberries (or you can substitute in black currants)
5 ounces of red grapes
Plenty of ice cubes

How to Make It:

Take the grapes off stalks before you use them. Wash all berries carefully. Push the blueberries, blackberries and grapes through a juice machine, keeping a few back for garnishes.

In a large glass, place plenty of ice cubes. Pour the juice over ice. Garnish the juice with the reserved berries.

Serve the juice right away. Makes a single serving.

Easy Orange Yogurt Smoothie Recipe

Oranges offer plenty of vitamin C and yogurt offers important live cultures that your body needs. This smoothie is delicious, creamy and refreshing. It's so tasty that you may want to drink it as a dessert. Make sure the ingredients are well chilled to get a cool smoothie that is wonderful, especially on a hot day.

What You'll Need:

1 cup of low fat yogurt with live cultures
1 ½ cups of raspberries, well washed and chilled
1 ¼ cups of orange juice, preferably fresh squeezed, chilled

How to Make It:

In a blender, add the yogurt and raspberries. Blend until you have a creamy, smooth mixture. Place orange juice in the blender with the yogurt, raspberry mixture. Blend for about 30 seconds more or until the orange juice is incorporated.

Pour the blender contents into two large glasses. Serve quickly while the smoothie is chilled. Makes two servings.

Chapter 9: Detox Diet Snack and Appetizer Recipes

Easy Mint Salsa Recipe

This salsa is given a boost with the addition of mint, which is known to include two phytochemicals that may help to prevent cancer. All the ingredients in the salsa are great additions to your detox plan as well. Enjoy serving this salsa with pita chips or some veggies. Add leftovers to poultry, fish or tofu dishes.

What You'll Need:

1 medium red onion, minced
1 jalapeno pepper, seeds removed and minced
1 mango, diced
1 lime, juiced
2 medium sized tomatoes, diced
Salt to taste
2/3 cup of fresh mint, chopped
Dash of cayenne pepper

How to Make It:

Combine together the onion, mango and tomatoes. Add the lime juice and jalapeno pepper, tossing to coat with lime juice. Add in fresh mint, dash of cayenne pepper and a bit of salt to taste. Mix well. Serve immediately or allow to chill before serving. Makes four servings of salsa.

Seed and Nut Veggie Dip Recipe

Nuts are a great way to get healthy fats and protein while you are following a detox diet. This combination of nuts makes a delicious dip that adds plenty of flavor and some protein to veggies. Dip carrots, celery and other veggies in the dip for a healthy, filling snack. All the flavors from the dip will add something special to raw veggies.

What You'll Need:

1 tablespoon of dried thyme
1/3 cup of sesame seeds
¼ teaspoon of black pepper, freshly ground
1/3 cup of roasted cashews, unsalted and chopped finely
3 tablespoons of coriander seeds
¼ teaspoon of salt
2 tablespoons of cumin seeds
¼ teaspoon of chili powder

How to Make It:

Heat a small saucepan on medium heat. When warm, add in sesame seeds, toasting them for about two minutes. Seeds should be browned lightly. Put the sesame seeds in a small bowl, sitting aside. Separately, roast the cumin and coriander seeds on medium, tossing while roasting. Allow them to cooking until just barely browned. Put the coriander and cumin seeds in a small bowl where they can cool.

Add cumin and coriander seeds to a coffee or spice grinder, grinding them until well ground. Place ground cumin and coriander in a bowl, adding the thyme, chili, sesame seeds, salt, cashews and pepper. Combine together thoroughly. Place in an airtight container for storage. Makes about a cup of the nut dip.

Crispy, Healthy Kale Chip Recipe

Kale is one of the healthiest greens and is rich in dietary fiber and important nutrients. It's a great addition to a detox diet. Turning kale into chips gives you a deliciously crunchy snack that will keep you from reaching from chips or other unhealthy foods. Have fun trying these chips with different combinations of spices for variety.

What You'll Need:

Olive oil
Sea salt
Spices of choice
1-2 kale bunches

How to Make It:

Preheat the oven to 425F.

Take kale off its stalk, only leaving the greens. Break greens into big pieces. Place the pieces of kale into a large bowl. Slowly drizzle with a bit of olive oil, using your hands to rub the oil into all the kale. Add your spices of choice and a bit of sea salt.

Spray a large cookie sheet with nonstick cooking spray.

Take the kale and spread it out on the sheet in a single layer. Place kale in the oven, allowing to bake for about 5 minutes. Once it begins to brown, flip kale over, allowing it to bake on the other side for another 4-5 minutes.

While baking, carefully watch the kale. Since it is fairly thin, it can begin burning quickly. Remove kale from the oven, serving right away. Leftover chips can be stored in a plastic container or plastic ziplock bag.

Note: Some great spices to try with the kale chips include garam masala, cumin, curry or a nice chili blend

Coconut Chocolate Homemade Energy Bars

While it's possible to buy energy bars, homemade options are made only with ingredients you decide to put into them. Making your own bars allows you to adapt the bars to your taste and in most cases, it's a cheaper way to enjoy energy bars as well. If you're craving chocolate, these bars combine together coconut and chocolate for plenty of wonderful flavor.

What You'll Need:

½ cup of raw walnuts
2 tablespoons of raw cacao powder
1 cup of dates, whole and pitted
2 tablespoons of shredded coconut, unsweetened
½ cup of raw almonds

How to Make It:

Place the dates in a food processor, processing them until you have a chunky, coarse paste. Add the walnuts and the almonds to the processor, continuing to process until the nuts are in small pieces. Place nut and date mixture in a medium bowl. Add the cacao and the coconut to the bowl, mixing well.

To make the bars, grab some of the mix, pressing it together and creating a large ball. After you have a nice, sticky ball, begin to roll the ball out into a roll that is about two inches wide. On a prepared baking sheet, press and form the roll, making it into the shape of a bar.

Roll bars in a bit more of the coconut, which makes them look great and also keeps them from sticking together as much. Wrap bars with plastic wrap, storing them in the refrigerator. Enjoy any time. Makes about six bars, depending on the size you make the bars.

Chapter 10: Detox Diet Dessert Recipes

Homemade Chocolate Pudding Recipe

This recipe is inspired by the recipe from "The Great American Detox Diet," written by Alex Jamieson. It allows you to enjoy delicious chocolate flavor while sticking to raw foods that go well with any detox diet. This pudding is so tasty, you may want to whip up a double batch.

What You'll Need:

2 tablespoons of raw nut butter
10 fresh dates, pitted and then cut up into chunks
1 teaspoon of vanilla
2 tablespoons of unsweetened cocoa powder
1 ½ - 2 cups of filtered water
10 dried figs, without stems and cut into chunks

How to Make It:

In a blender or a food processor, add the nut butter, figs, vanilla, 1 cup of the water, dates and cocoa. Begin pulsing to start breaking up the fruit. As the fruits begin breaking down, start blending more until you have a cream, smooth mixture. You can add more water if you need to, ensuring you get the consistency you prefer for your pudding. Makes 2.5 cups of pudding.

Detox Pumpkin Pie Recipe

Pumpkin is so good for you and you can create a pumpkin pie that makes a delicious, yet nutritious dessert. This recipe allows you to enjoy all the goodness of pumpkin the vegan way. This is a perfect recipe choice to try while you are following a detox diet.

What You'll Need:

1 teaspoon of cinnamon
1 tablespoon of safflower or coconut oil
5 tablespoons of rice flour
¼ teaspoon of ground cloves
1 ½ teaspoons of baking powder
4 tablespoons of water
¾ cup of brown rice syrup
½ teaspoon of ginger
16 ounces of natural pumpkin
½ cup of water
½ teaspoon of salt

How to Make It:

Prepare your own all natural pie crust recipe or purchase an organic, natural pie crust to use for the recipe.

Preheat the oven to 375F.

Stir together the oil, 4 tablespoons of water and the rice flour until you have a thick paste. Add together the rest of the ingredients, leaving out the baking powder, and mix the ingredients together thoroughly. Fold in the baking powder.

Pour the pumpkin filling into the pie crush right away. Place pie on a baking sheet, placing in the oven and baking for 25 minutes. After 25 minutes, the temperature should be lowered to 350F. Allow the pumpkin pie to continue baking for about 45 more minutes. The pie should be firm and golden on top when it is done.

Allow to cool. Serve while still warm or chill and serve cold. Makes one 9-inch pumpkin pie.

Easy Natural Fudge (No Sugar) Recipe

When you went on the detox diet, you may have thought that sweets were gone for good. This recipes allows you to indulge in fudge without the guilt. In fact, this no sugar recipe uses great ingredients that go along with your detox diet. The raw cacao added to the fudge has many health benefits, so it allows you to enjoy the rich chocolate flavor, even while following a detox lifestyle.

What You'll Need:

½ cup of virgin coconut oil, organic
1 teaspoon of vanilla
1 cup of cacao powder, raw organic
½ cup of maple syrup
¼ cup of shredded coconut, unsweetened

How to Make It:

In a medium-sized bowl, combine the ingredients together. Mix well until you have a smooth mixture. Press the fudge mixture into a baking pans or roll into small balls. Place in the refrigerator, allowing to set for at least two hours. Makes about eight squares or balls of fudge.

Note: To add extra nutrition and some variety, you can also add in processed dates, Maca powder, soaked and processed almonds, coconut milk

Delicious Peach Bake Dessert Recipe

Peaches are a sweet juicy fruit that can easily be made into a delectable recipe. For the best flavor, try this recipe with peaches in the summer, which is when you will find peaches to be at their most fragrant and juiciest. When you bake the peaches, you will really bring out their wonderful flavor. The addition of honey and apple juice really makes this recipe a special dessert dish that your whole family will enjoy.

What You'll Need:

2 teaspoons of almond extract
3 tablespoons of fresh apple juice
4 fresh peaches, well ripened
3 tablespoons of clear honey
Low fat yogurt with live cultures for serving

How to Make It:

Preheat the oven to 375F.

Cut peaches in half, twisting them to help eliminate the pits from the peaches. You should have eight peach halves when you are done.

Prepare a large roasting pan with nonstick cooking spray. Place the peaches in the roasting pan, leaving their cut sides facing upwards. Mix together the almond extract, honey and apple juice in a little bowl. After well mixed, pour the juice mix over the peaches, making sure they are evenly covered.

Place peaches in the oven, allowing them to bake for about 25 minutes. Peaches should be tender. Set out four serving plates. On each plate, put two of the peach halves. Drizzle the peaches with the juices left in the pans. Add a spoonful or two of yogurt on the side. Serve while peaches are still warm. Makes four servings.

Poached Honeyed Pears Recipe

Pears contain both potassium and vitamin C, which are important nutrients for the body. The provide delicate flavor and their wonderful sweetness can be easily turned into a wonderful dessert that will help you stick to your detox diet. The lavender may be unexpected, but it adds a wonderful flavor and makes an elegant garnish for this dish.

What You'll Need:

4 large, firm pears
1 cup of water
3 tablespoons of clear honey
1 cinnamon stick
1 lemon, juiced
2-3 dried lavender heads
Small pinch of saffron threads

How to Make It:

In a heavy pan that is just large enough for the pears, heat up the lemon juice and the honey. Gently stir on low heat until the honey completely dissolves. Add the flowers from 1-2 of the heads of lavender, the cinnamon stick, saffron threads and the water to the pan. Allow the mixture to come to a boil. Once boiling, reduce heat, allowing the mixture to gently simmer for about five minutes.

Meanwhile, peel pears, allowing their stalks to stay attached. After honey mixture has simmered for five minutes, place pears in the pan, allowing them to simmer for about 20-25 minutes. Turn the pears from time to time, basting them with the juices. Make sure pears are completely tender before removing from the heat.

Let the pears cool, serving them when they have reached room temperature. Add a few lavender flowers to the plates of pears as a garnish. Makes four servings.

Chapter 11: Detox Diet 7 Day Meal Plan

Day 1:

Breakfast:

- Vegetarian breakfast patties
- Fruit of choice
- Delicious Strawberry Smoothie

Lunch:

- Gazpacho soup recipe
- Side salad

Dinner:

- Vegetarian Black Bean Burgers topped with tomatoes and lettuce

Snack:

- Crispy Healthy Kale Chips

Day 2:

Breakfast:

- Detox Friendly Buckwheat Pancakes topped with fruit of choice
- Delicious Green Cleansing Juice

Lunch:

- Detox Minestrone Soup served over brown rice

Dinner:

- Red Snapper and Kale
- Burdock Carrot Stir-fry

Snack:

- Coconut Chocolate Homemade Energy Bar

Day 3:

Breakfast:

- Easy Herbed Egg Omelet
- Piece of fruit

- Tropical Pineapple Smoothie

Lunch:

- Black Bean Chili
- Cleansing seaweed salad

Dinner:

- Salmon Fillets with Orange Glaze
- Tasty Roasted Roots

Snack:

- Homemade Chocolate Pudding

Day 4:

Breakfast:

- Apple Nut Oatmeal
- Tasty Berry Juice

Lunch:

- Tuscan Veggie Bean Soup
- Side salad

Dinner:

- Tasty Green Leaf Lettuce Wraps

Snack:

- Delicious Peach Bake Dessert

Day 5:

Breakfast:

- Date Porridge
- Easy Orange Yogurt Smoothie

Lunch:

- Grapefruit and Sesame Salad

Dinner:

- Wild Rice and Chicken
- Steamed broccoli
- Side salad

Snack:

- Easy Mint Salsa with veggies

Day 6:

Breakfast:

- Homemade Apple Cinnamon Granola
- Piece of fruit
- Delicious Strawberry Smoothie

Lunch:

- Leftover Tasty Green Leaf Lettuce Wraps

Dinner:

- Easy Stir Fried Veggies and Fish

Snack:

- Raw veggies of choice with Seed and Nut Veggie Dip

Day 7:

Breakfast:

- Vegetarian breakfast patties
- Small bowl of chopped fruit (apples, strawberries, blueberries and pineapple)

Lunch:

- Delicious Lemon Dressed Kale Salad

Dinner:

- Lemon Rosemary Chicken Recipe
- Green Beans
- Side Salad

Snack:

- Cacao Powder Smoothie

Section 2: DASH Diet

The DASH Diet is an important strategy for anyone who wants to lower their blood pressure and improve their overall health without dealing with risky medications and their side effects. This simple diet focuses on low fat, low cholesterol foods and natural ingredients, making it inexpensive and easy to follow. Plus, you'll be surprised by how delicious heart healthy foods can be. If you've been warned about the possible dangers of high blood pressure and a normal North American diet, it's time to make some changes.

The recipes contained in this book don't encompass the entire range of DASH diet options, but they will give you an idea of how you can change your favorite foods to fit the diet plan. In general, they focus on reducing the fat, cholesterol and refined carbohydrates in a dish without losing out on flavor. If you've experienced too many flavorless health foods, these recipes could be the solution that you've been hoping for.

What Is the DASH Diet?

DASH is a term that stands for "Dietary Approaches to Stop Hypertension." It is designed to be a lifestyle change for people who want to treat or prevent hypertension, also known as high blood pressure. The diet is based on studies originally performed by the US National Institutes of Health that examined three different dietary plans and their effects on blood pressure. The result is a plan that focuses on increased consumption of plant foods such as nuts, beans, low fat dairy products, vegetables and fruit.

This diet plan is recommended by the National Heart, Lung and Blood Institute for anyone who wants to decrease their blood pressure and improve heart health. In studies performed on the diet, people who followed it showed a systolic blood pressure reduction of 6mm Hg, as well as a diastolic blood pressure reduction of 3 mm Hg in patients who had tested in the high-normal range, also called pre-hypertension. In patients who had existing hypertension, the diet caused reductions of 11 mm Hg and 6 mm Hg respectively, with no change in body weight. While it was not designed for weight loss, the DASH diet's focus on lower calorie, healthier foods does make it a viable choice for people who want to reduce their body fat levels.

What Is Hypertension and Why Is It Dangerous?

Hypertension, or high blood pressure, refers to the force your blood puts on the walls of your arteries. Doctors measure it in millimeters of mercury, or mm Hg, and record it as two different numbers. They measure both the systolic blood pressure, or the pressure when your heart is beating, and the diastolic blood pressure, or the pressure between beats. A person's blood pressure can rise and fall over the course of a given day, but continued high levels can be very dangerous to your health.

When your blood flows with a lot of force, it can damage the veins and arteries, as well as organs like the eyes, heart, kidneys and brain. Most people who develop high blood pressure have difficulty lowering it. Left uncontrolled, this condition can lead to blindness, kidney and heart disease, and even stroke. About one in three people have high blood pressure, but many aren't aware of the problem.

Many doctors and patients turn to medication at the

first sign of high blood pressure, but this technique might not be the right one for you. Many blood pressure treatments have dehydrating effects. Others can induce depression or extreme tiredness. The very low blood pressure that is caused by some drugs can also result in severe dizziness and a tingling feeling in your fingers and toes. In more serious cases, these drugs can cause insomnia, pain in the feet, weakness and leg cramps, or an irregular heartbeat. That's a lot of risk to take when you could address the problem through less intrusive methods like diet and exercise.

How Does the DASH Diet Work?

The DASH diet provides an alternative to conventional, drug-based methods of controlling blood pressure. It is designed to help you maintain a healthy weight with moderate levels of physical activity. It focuses on reducing sodium levels, which have been shown to elevate blood pressure in some people. It also includes decreased levels of saturated fat and cholesterol, which contribute to narrowing of the arteries and can make it hard for blood to cycle properly.

Over time, this diet can help patients who have high blood pressure lower their levels and reduce their medication requirements. In some cases, it can even allow you to discontinue use of medication entirely. It is important to change your dosages only on the recommendation of a doctor, however. Don't stop using your high blood pressure medicine just because you've started using the DASH diet.

DASH Study Daily Nutrient Goals

The studies used to formulate the DASH diet set a few standard daily nutrient goals, which are also used in the main plan. Following this diet means trying to keep your total fat intake to about 27 percent of your daily calories. Saturated fat should make up only about 6 percent of your calories, however. The DASH diet is relatively high in carbohydrates, which should make up about 55 percent of your daily calorie intake, but most of the carbohydrates you eat should be complex ones, rather than those derived from white flour and sugar.

The DASH diet also recommends trying to keep your daily cholesterol intake below 150 milligrams. The original studies aimed for a sodium intake of 2,300 milligrams or less, but more recent research suggests that 1,500 milligrams or less is even better for reducing blood pressure. It's a good idea to get at least 30 g of fiber and 1,250 milligrams of calcium each day while on this diet, as well.

DASH Diet Guidelines

All those number can be hard to understand, so the researchers who wrote the DASH diet plan broke it down into clearer recommendations. They suggest eating six to eight servings of whole grain per day, four to five servings of vegetables, and four to five servings of fruit. Consuming two to three servings of low fat dairy products provides protein and calcium. If you eat meat, aim to consume six or fewer one-ounce servings of lean meat, poultry or fish per day. Vegetarians can substitute an egg for one serving of meat.

The DASH diet guidelines recommend consuming four to five servings of nuts, legumes and seeds per week, though vegetarians should increase these to replace meat. Fats and oils should be kept to a relative minimum of two to three servings per day. This includes, mayonnaise, margarine and salad dressings. Sweets need to be eaten in moderation; the DASH diet recommends having five low-fat servings or fewer every week. Very active people can increase servings of grain, fruits and vegetables, low fat dairy and lean meat to help support their higher metabolisms.

Using DASH for Weight Loss

The DASH diet wasn't originally designed to help people lose weight, but it can be adapted to help you maintain a healthier weight and reduce your risk of high blood pressure. Doctors recommend simply using the lower calorie recommendations for the diet to cut back your energy intake. Eat a little less than you normally would and focus on getting about 30 to 60 minutes of regular physical activity, like walking or swimming, every day. Your weight may not decrease dramatically, but it should drop slowly over a longer period of time. Experts recommend this kind of loss because it is the most likely to be permanent.

Intuitive Eating with the DASH Diet

While many people like to start out counting their calories to ensure they're getting the right level of nutrition on the DASH diet, this doesn't work for everyone. If you have trouble with calorie counting, or if you've been on the diet long enough to know your choices are good ones, it might be time to look at intuitive eating. This technique involves paying attention to the signals your body is sending. When you've mastered intuitive eating, you'll provide food when your body is hungry, stop eating when it sends signals of fullness, and avoid snacking for emotional reasons or out of boredom. This method can be very helpful for people who tend to have trouble with more mathematical techniques, but it does take some practice.

Intuitive eating is compatible with the DASH diet from the beginning, but you'll need to modify your strategy a little bit. Start out by focusing on the low calorie foods that are acceptable on this diet. That means consuming more fruit and raw, non-starchy vegetables while eating more calorically-dense foods in small amounts. Even if you have a craving for nuts, beef or cheese, try having just a few bites to begin with. You may be able to conquer your craving quickly without overeating.

Making DASH Dieting Easy

The transition period between a normal North American diet and the DASH technique can be a rocky one, especially if you don't know how to find tasty snacks or eat at your favorite restaurants. Make things simpler by keeping pre-cut fresh fruit, vegetables and low-calorie dairy snacks in your refrigerator at all times. That way, when you want to grab something simple, they'll be right at your fingertips.

Make eating out on the DASH diet easier by turning the menu into a treasure hunt. You may be surprised by how many healthy foods you can find. Most restaurants now offer a veggie burger instead of a beef burger. You may also be able to choose steamed vegetables or fresh fruit rather than French fries or onion rings. Choose a garden salad with a light oil and vinegar dressing in restaurants that don't offer many vegetable options, and be sure to take part of your meal home. You'll find eating out on the DASH diet much simpler than you expected.

Last, but not least, practice sneaking DASH foods into your ordinary meals. It's easy to add cucumber slices, shredded cabbage or carrots to an ordinary sandwich. If you usually consume tea or coffee, add a full glass of skim milk to it to boost protein without increasing your cholesterol. Vegetable broths and fruit purees provide a great way to ensure you're getting all your fruits and veggies: just drink them!

Exercise and the DASH Diet

The DASH diet works well on its own, but when paired with exercise, it has considerably better effects. In one study of 124 men and women over the age of 50, 30 minutes of aerobic exercise three times per week lower blood pressure and weight much more quickly than diet alone. If you need to make lifestyle changes in order to improve your blood pressure and reduce your BMI, adding light to moderate physical activity is the best way to do it.

The process is very simple. Just add a half hour of swimming, walking or other activity to your day at least three times per week. The workout doesn't need to be severe. In fact, you should be able to hold a conversation while you're getting your exercise. Try to recruit a workout buddy to help keep you on track and develop healthy habits. You'll soon be feeling lighter and more energetic. You'll even develop more stamina, making it easier to stay active.

Recipes for the DASH Diet

These recipes are adapted from books and online sources. They range from very simple to multi-step preparations for fancier occasions, but you don't have to be a master chef to prepare them. While several of them rely on slightly unusual ingredients, you should be able to find these at many standard grocery stores. Consider checking the ethnic or natural foods section for low-sodium soy sauce, chili paste and other less common ingredients. The extra flavor they give to your meals makes it worthwhile to seek these foods out.

You don't have to jump straight into preparing just DASH diet recipes, either. You can incorporate a few of these dishes into your normal routine, increasing them until you're eating healthy all week long. That's what makes the DASH diet such a good idea. It helps you make healthy decisions and incorporate them into your life without having to turn your normal way of eating upside down. If you care about the health of your heart, arteries and brain, it may be time to try out some of these great DASH recipes. In just a little while, you won't know how you ever lived without them.

Appetizers

DASH Spinach Dip

This cheesy dip eliminates the cholesterol-laden cream cheese and full-fat sour cream normally used in spinach dips, substituting velvety Great Northern beans and low fat dairy. Instead of heavily-salted ingredients, it relies on flavorful herbs and garlic to add interest. The result is a creamy dip that doesn't taste like health food. It makes a great choice for parties and goes well with sliced vegetables or warm, crusty bread.

Ingredients

2 pounds fresh spinach or 3 packages frozen spinach
1 pound or one can cooked Great Northern beans
½ cup low fat sour cream
2 tablespoons Parmesan cheese
2 tablespoons fresh parsley
1 tablespoon fresh basil
2 teaspoons black pepper
2 cloves fresh garlic

Wash and drain the fresh spinach or thaw and drain if you are using frozen products. Drain the beans and mash or puree until smooth. Combine all ingredients and stir until well combined, then pour into an oven-safe dish. Bake at 350 degrees Fahrenheit for about 30 minutes or until the mixture is hot throughout and bubbly.

Stuffed Portabella Mushrooms

Stuffed mushrooms are a classic appetizer, but they too-frequently contain cholesterol-packed bacon, cream cheese, eggs and other health-hazard ingredients. This version uses fresh spinach combined with garlic, tarragon and strongly-flavored cheese to provide excitement without the fat. The make-ahead element of these stuffed mushrooms means they're the perfect last-minute choice when you have company or just don't want to spend too much time in the kitchen

Ingredients

4 large portabella mushrooms
1 cup fresh or frozen spinach
4 teaspoons grated Parmesan cheese
1 tablespoon fresh tarragon
2 teaspoons olive oil
2 cloves fresh garlic
½ teaspoon black pepper

Crush the garlic and remove the stems from the portabella mushrooms. Chop the stems finely. Drain the spinach thoroughly. Heat 1 teaspoon of olive oil over medium-high heat in a heavy pan and sauté the garlic, pepper and tarragon for one minute. Add the mushroom stems and spinach leaves to the pan, sautéing 3 to 4 minutes or until stems are tender. Remove and place in a bowl. Add remaining 1 teaspoon of olive oil to the pan and place the mushrooms in the pan, cap-side down. Saute for 3 minutes without stirring or turning.

Flip the caps, cover, and reduce heat to low for another 2 minutes. Remove and place the caps on a foil-lined baking sheet with the gills facing up. Fill each mushroom with ¼ of the spinach mixture. Top with Parmesan cheese. If you are making the recipe ahead, cover the sheet with plastic wrap and place it in the refrigerator or freezer until ready to serve. Otherwise, place the mushrooms on a rack 6 inches below your broiler and cook for 3 to 4 minutes, until the cheese has just browned.

Crispy Coconut Chicken Fingers

Coconut shrimp is a perennial favorite, but it's also loaded with saturated fat and cholesterol. This healthier alternative uses chicken thighs to offer just as much flavor in a better-for-you package. Combined with the sweet and spicy dipping sauce, this recipe will be a hit at your next party. Vegetarians and vegans can also enjoy this dish; just substitute tempeh for the chicken and egg replacement powder for the egg white as preferred.

Ingredients

½ pound boneless, skinless chicken thighs
¼ cup no-sodium bread crumbs
¼ cup unsweetened coconut flakes
1 teaspoon powdered garlic
1 egg white
¼ teaspoon black pepper
Dipping Sauce
2 tablespoons orange marmalade
1 ½ teaspoons rice vinegar or lemon juice
¼ teaspoon cayenne pepper

Wash the chicken and pat it dry. Slice into 20 individual bite-sized pieces. Combine the bread crumbs, coconut, garlic and black pepper in a small bowl. Beat egg white thoroughly. Dip each piece of chicken into the egg, then roll in the bread crumb mixture. Place on a lightly-oiled baking sheet and bake at 425 degrees for 10 minutes. Flip each piece, then return the sheet to the oven for another 10 minutes.

Combine all sauce ingredients in a small bowl and stir to combine. Arrange the chicken bites on a platter around the bowl of sauce and serve right away.

Vegetable Sushi

When you mention sushi, most people assume raw fish or eggs will be involved, but the term "sushi" actually refers to the slightly sour rice. You can top this delicate Japanese food with all kinds of ingredients, including fresh and colorful vegetables. Use brown rice to add more fiber and a nutty flavor. You can mix and match the vegetables in this recipe, making it an excellent choice to use up leftovers.

Ingredients

1 cup short grain brown rice
1 1/2 cups water
1 tablespoon plain rice vinegar
1 package sushi nori seaweed sheets
Vegetables
steamed or roasted asparagus spears
avocado
roasted beets
fresh cucumber strips
pickled daikon or radish
shredded kale
roasted sweet potatoes
roasted kale
fresh or sautéed mushrooms

thin slices of tomato

Place the brown rice in a pan or rice cooker brown and rinse until the water runs clear. Drain and add 1 ½ cups of water. Cook until the rice is tender. Sprinkle with vinegar and add salt substitute to taste. Stir with a wide, flat spoon or a rice paddle and allow the mixture to cool.

To assemble, place one sheet of nori on a bamboo sushi mat. Spoon approximately ½ cup of the cooked rice mixture in a thin layer across the whole piece of nori. Place shredded kale, asparagus stalks, cucumber strips or other vegetables on top of the rice, then roll the seaweed over the vegetables and into a long log, using the mat to keep it intact. Place the finished roll seam-side-down on a cutting board and slice into pieces with a very sharp knife. Serve immediately with pickled ginger, low sodium soy sauce, horseradish or sesame seeds.

Fresh Mushroom Quesadillas

Mushroom quesadillas are a popular dish in Mexico, where they are referred to as quesadillas de hongo. Unlike processed American versions of Hispanic cuisine, this dish is light and healthy without being dull or flavorless. Say goodbye to fatty, uniform Mexican fast food and hello to healthy flavor with these spicy but savory tortillas.

Ingredients

1 pound fresh mushrooms
1 medium onion
1 cup shredded Swiss cheese
¼ cup low fat sour cream
3 cloves garlic
2 tablespoons fresh cilantro
1 fresh jalapeno pepper
1 teaspoon olive oil
1 package low sodium, whole grain flour or corn tortillas

Finely chop mushrooms, onion, jalapeno, cilantro and garlic. Heat 1 teaspoon of olive oil in a heavy pan over medium heat and sauté the alliums and mushrooms for about 10 minutes, or until tender and lightly browned. Season with black pepper to taste. Heat a large skillet to medium-low and place a single tortilla on the surface, flipping to warm throughout. Sprinkle with cheese, chopped jalapeno and cilantro. Allow the cheese to melt, then spoon on a small amount of the mushroom mixture. Add a second tortilla and flip the entire quesadilla over. Remove to a plate to cool and repeat until you have used all the cheese and mushroom mixture. Slice each quesadilla into quarters or eighths, depending on the size of your tortilla. Serve warm with low fat sour cream.

Beverages

Peanut Butter and Banana Smoothie

Whether you'd like to enjoy a smoothie for breakfast, dessert or a between-meal treat, this one is a great choice. The banana provides plenty of natural sweetness, while the peanut butter offers monounsaturated "healthy" fats and protein. Combined with non-fat milk, this could be the perfect pick me up when you're feeling tired. Vegans can substitute unsweetened soy or almond milk.

Ingredients

1 cup skim milk
1 medium banana
1 tablespoon creamy natural peanut butter, unsalted

Peel and slice the banana. Place in a blender or food processor and add the milk and peanut butter. Process until completely smooth. For a more milkshake-like version, freeze the banana before blending.

No-Booze Margarita

Most people on the DASH diet need to take alcohol in moderation, while some need to eschew it completely. This tasty beverage offers the same overall flavor as a margarita, but without the alcohol. That means you can drink it at any time!

Ingredients

2 cups ice
½ cup lime juice
2 tablespoons simple syrup
Sliced limes for garnish
Simple Syrup (makes 6 tablespoons):
¼ cup raw sugar
¼ cup water

Combine the water and sugar in a small saucepan over medium heat, stirring until the sugar has dissolved completely. Remove to a sealed container and refrigerate for up to a week.

Combine syrup, ice and lime juice in a blender or powerful food processor. Process until a smooth slush has formed. Pour into a chilled glass and garnish with lime slices.

Sugar-free Agua Fresca

Aguas fresca, sweet non-carbonated beverages popular in Mexico and the southeastern US, can be a refreshing choice for hot days. Unfortunately, most of these drinks contain large quantities of white refined sugar. This variation uses fresh fruit to provide the sweetness, making it a much healthier and lower-calorie option you can enjoy more often.

Ingredients

3 pounds watermelon
½ cup unsweetened cranberry juice
½ cup apple juice
¼ cup lime juice
1 lime

Remove the seeds and rind from the watermelon, cutting it into fine dice. Place it in a food processor or blender and process until a smooth puree is produced. Sieve this puree to remove the excess pulp, yielding a clear, delicious juice. Cut the lime into thin slices. In a large pitcher, combine the watermelon juice, cranberry juice, apple juice and lime juice. Stir to combine completely. The mixture may be slightly cloudy, but it will taste delicious when refrigerated and garnished with a slice of fresh lime.

Spicy, Sweet and Tangy Herbal Tea

Technically a tisane, because no tea leaves are involved in its brewing, this drink can be served either warm or chilled. It uses only natural, unprocessed sweeteners, making it an excellent alternative to sodas and conventional iced tea beverages.

Ingredients

1 ½ quarts water
½ cup fresh mint
1/3 cup lemon juice
3/8 cup strongly-flavored honey
4 tablespoons fresh ginger
1 medium lemon

Peel and chop the ginger. Slice the lemon thinly into rounds. Combine the ginger, water and lemon juice in a saucepan and bring to a boil over high heat. Reduce to low and allow to simmer for 5 minutes. Add the mint, remove from heat entirely, and allow to steep for 5 to 8 minutes. Use a fine sieve to remove the mint leaves and ginger, which can be discarded after use. Stir in the honey and serve warm or cold with a lemon slice floating on top.

Non-Alcoholic Hurricane Punch

Traditionally made with rum, this beverage is a great choice to add lots of vitamin C and other antioxidants to your diet. When made with ice, it becomes a delicious frosty drink that's perfect for a hot summer day.

Ingredients

2 cups or 1 can fresh unsweetened pineapple
1 orange
1 lemon
1 lime
½ cup unsweetened cranberry juice
1 cup ice (optional)

Peel the citrus fruit and set aside. Chop the pineapple roughly into chunks and combine in a blender with the cranberry juice and citrus. Add the ice if you are using it and process until the mixture is a smooth liquid or frosty puree. Serve in tall glasses with a spoon for the icy version.

Breakfast

Chewy Fruit Bars

This simple bar is sweet and hearty, making it the perfect choice for breakfast on the go. Unlike many ordinary granola bars, it's not high in fats or refined sugars, however. Natural ingredients such as multigrain cereal and bran help keep the glycemic index low, while walnuts, dried fruit and almond butter provide the energy your body needs to keep going. Enjoy these bars as a quick snack or even a light dessert in a pinch.

2 cups dry whole grain hot cereal
1 cup bran flakes cereal
¾ cup honey
¾ cup low salt almond butter
½ cup non-fat dry milk
½ cup dried apricot pieces
½ cup dried cranberries
½ cup walnut pieces
1 tablespoon canola or light olive oil
1 tablespoon vanilla extract

In a large bowl, combine cereals, nuts, dried fruit and dry milk. Place almond butter, honey and oil in a small saucepan and heat to medium-low, stirring constantly. Allow mixture to bubble, then remove the pan from the heat and add vanilla extract. Pour this mixture over the fruit and cereal, stirring until completely combined. Grease a baking pan with canola oil or line it with parchment paper. Spread the mixture into the pan, patting it down tightly. Bake for 20 minutes at 325 degrees and set aside to cool on a rack for 20 minutes or until firm. Cut into 12 pieces and store in an air-tight container at room temperature.

Broiled Almond-Banana Toast

Bananas are a classic breakfast ingredient, but on their own they tend to be carbohydrate-heavy and unsatisfying. That's why this morning treat pairs fresh banana with fiber-rich whole grain toast and protein-packed almond butter. Putting the finished product under the broiler caramelizes the natural sugars in the banana, producing a delicious, gooey result that you'll also enjoy as a snack.

Ingredients

2 slices whole grain bread
2 tablespoons smooth almond butter
1 small banana
ground cinnamon and nutmeg to taste

Toast the bread and arrange it on an oven-safe plate or a small baking sheet. Spread each slice with 1 tablespoon of almond butter. Slice the banana into rounds of medium thickness and arrange them on top of the almond butter. Sprinkle the surface with cinnamon and nutmeg, then place under the broiler for 2 to 3 minutes, or until the almond butter melts slightly and the bananas begin to brown. Allow to cool and eat with your fingers, or dig in right away with a fork.

DASH-friendly Oatmeal

Oatmeal naturally has properties that make it good for your heart, but many commercial instant products contain large amounts of sugar, sodium and other unhealthy ingredients. If you love a hot, hearty bowl of oats in the morning, this low-cholesterol, salt-free option will satisfy you without cutting back on taste. Fresh fruit and nuts add to the oatmeal's flavor and nutrition profile, making this a breakfast recipe you're sure to love. Try it out on a cold winter morning.

Ingredients

1 ½ cups unsweetened almond milk
1 cup old fashioned rolled oats
¾ cup mixed berries or other chopped fruit
1/8 cup whole pecans
¼ teaspoon vanilla extract
Cinnamon to taste

Combine the almond milk and vanilla in a small sauce pan over medium-high heat. Bring to a gentle simmer and add the oats. Cook, stirring occasionally, for about 5 minutes or until almost all the liquid has been absorbed. Stir in the fruit and serve topped with pecans and cinnamon.

Healthy Homemade Granola

Traditional granolas are full of healthy ingredients such as whole grains, nuts and fruit, but they tend to be heavy on the fat, salt and added sugar. The situation gets worse in the case of some packaged granolas, which add preservatives and other artificial ingredients. This homemade granola recipe is nutritionally dense and concentrates on healthy fats and natural, relatively unrefined sources of sugar. Flax seeds add an extra omega-3 punch, making this recipe a great way to start your day.

Ingredients

3 cups old-fashioned rolled oats
1 cup sliced almonds
1 cup raisins or dried cranberries
4 tablespoons flax seed
¼ cup raw sugar
1/4 cup honey
¼ cup sunflower or canola oil
½ teaspoon vanilla extract
½ teaspoon ground sugar
½ teaspoon allspice
½ teaspoon ground ginger

Combine the oats, almonds, flax, spices and sugar in a large bowl, mixing thoroughly. In a separate bowl combine the honey, oil and vanilla extract. Pour the wet ingredient mixture into the dry ingredients, mixing with a spatula as you pour. Stir until the dry mixture is wet throughout. Lightly grease one to two cookie sheets with sunflower oil or another monounsaturated fat. Pour the wet granola into the pans, patting it into place if necessary. Bake in a 250 degree Fahrenheit oven for 90 minutes or until dry and lightly browned, stirring every 15 minutes. Break up chunks of granola as you stir to create the appropriate consistency. Allow the mixture to cool, then combine with the dried fruit and store in an air-tight container.

Toasted Breakfast Sandwich

Not every DASH-friendly breakfast recipe is sweet. There are also plenty of savory options that combine fresh vegetables with low-sodium, low-cholesterol proteins for a heartier start to your day. If you love eggs for breakfast, this recipe will help you enjoy them without the heart risk associated with large amounts of egg yolk. Flavorful mustard and tomatoes keep the open-faced sandwich interesting, so you won't miss the fat.

Ingredients

2 egg whites
½ cup fresh spinach leaves
1 slice whole grain bread
1 small tomato
1 ½ teaspoons olive oil
1 teaspoon prepared brown mustard
½ ounce slice reduced-fat cheddar cheese
Black pepper and paprika to taste

In a small pan, heat the olive oil to medium-high. Beat the egg whites and add to the hot oil, scrambling them until completely solid. Add the spinach and heat until wilted. Spread the mustard onto the bread and place it on an oven-safe plate or baking sheet. Arrange tomato slices on top of the mustard, then top with the egg mixture and thinly-sliced cheddar cheese. Sprinkle with black pepper and sharp paprika to taste. Bake in an oven or toaster oven at 400 degrees Fahrenheit until the bread is crisp and the cheese is melted and slightly browned.

Main Dishes

Simple Grilled Chicken

This basic chicken dish is easy to make on any outdoor grill. It combines the low cholesterol and white meat of bone-in chicken breasts with flavorful garlic and spices. The finished product is crisp, golden brown and caramelized for an intense flavor. You won't miss the extra fat!

Ingredients

4 bone-in chicken breasts with skin
2 cloves garlic
salt-free herb seasoning mix

Heat a gas or charcoal grill to medium heat. Fold non-stick aluminum foil into a boat shape for each chicken breast. Cut the garlic cloves in half and rub the cut surfaces over the skin of the chicken breasts. Sprinkle with seasoning mix to taste and place the chicken breasts in the boats, skin side down. Grill for 45 minutes or until the center reaches 160 degrees Fahrenheit, turning the chicken once every 10 to 15 minutes.

Basic Barbeque "Pork" Chops

Barbecued pork may sound unhealthy and decadent, but you can substitute other meats to make your favorite pork recipes compatible with the DASH diet. This recipe uses "chops" of boneless chicken thighs, since the dark meat provides similar flavor intensity to that of lean pork. Just make sure you don't overcook it, as the meat can easily dry out with too much heat. Add a fresh salad and this dish is ready to make a complete meal!

1 ½ pounds boneless chicken thighs
10 ounces low sodium condensed tomato soup
3 tablespoons red wine vinegar
2 tablespoons low sodium Worcestershire sauce
1 small onion
¾ cup water
1 teaspoon sharp paprika
1 teaspoon chili powder
¼ teaspoon cinnamon
¼ teaspoon black pepper
1/8 teaspoon cloves

Trim all fat from the chicken, cube, and set aside. Combine all other ingredients in a large bowl, then transfer to a large skillet with high sides. Heat to medium and add the chicken cubes, simmering for 30 minutes or until cooked thoroughly. Serve with bread or 2/3 cup of brown rice.

Miso-Marinated Cod

This spicy Asian fish recipe provides plenty of healthy polyunsaturated omega-3 fatty acids, along with the rich flavors of miso and chili paste. If cod is unavailable, use any firm, flaky white fish that can be cut into thick steaks. Avoid thin species like flounder, which will not cook correctly. While the marinade itself is very salty, the practice of wrapping the fish in a porous material prevents too much salt from getting into the food itself. To make this dish ahead, simply apply the marinade, then freeze the entire dish. Defrost slowly in the refrigerator before cooking normally.

Ingredients

1 pound cod
3 tablespoons low-salt sweet white miso
1 tablespoon garlic-chili paste
2 tablespoons apple juice
2 tablespoons unprocessed cane sugar, such as turbinado

Mix together all raw ingredients except for the fish. Take a piece of plastic wrap and spread it over the counter or a cutting board, then apply a layer of miso marinade a little larger than the total surface area of the fish. Place a piece of cheesecloth on top of the marinade layer. Wrap the cheesecloth around the fish, then apply marinade to the top side. Wrap the plastic around the fish and its wrapping, then place the plastic bundle into a freezer bag. Place in the refrigerator for two hours to overnight.

Remove the fish from the refrigerator and peel away the plastic and cheesecloth layers. Heat a large nonstick frying pan over medium heat and place the fish in it. Cook on both sides until the fish is opaque and flaky throughout. Serve with low-sodium miso soup, rice and Japanese pickles. Discard any unused marinade for safety reasons.

Blackened Beef

Thinly sliced lean top round beef seared with strong spices makes for an exciting and flavorful main dish, especially when you pair it with stewed potatoes, onions and carrots. Finish the dish with tender greens for a recipe that's tasty and nutritious. This blackened beef dish is especially good with crusty low-sodium bread.

Ingredients

1 pound lean top round of beef
6 medium red potatoes
4 large onions
3 large carrots
2 cups low-sodium beef broth
2 cups water
2 cloves garlic
1 bunch kale
2 tablespoons sharp paprika
1 tablespoon dried oregano
1 teaspoon chili powder
1 teaspoon powdered garlic
½ teaspoon black pepper
¼ teaspoon red pepper
¼ teaspoon mustard powder

Place the beef in the freezer until partially frozen. Cut the potatoes into quarters, mince the garlic cloves, slice the carrots into rounds and remove the stems from the kale. Chop the onions very finely to yield about 4 cups. Combine paprika, oregano, garlic powder, chili powder, red and black peppers and dry mustard in a small bowl with a lid. Set aside. Remove beef from freezer and slice it across the grain in strips about 1/8 inch thick. Sprinkle with the seasoning mix, covering all available surfaces. Lightly grease a large heavy skillet or stockpot then preheat over high. Add the meat strips and sear, stirring continuously, for about 5 minutes.

Add the broth and water to the pan to deglaze, then add potatoes and garlic to the skillet. Allow the blackened spices to float to the top. Cover and lower heat to medium, cooking for about 20 minutes or until potatoes are tender. Add the carrots and place the kale on top of the dish. Cover and cook for an additional 10 minutes. This dish can be served right from the skillet or pot.

Feta-ricotta Greek Pizza

Many DASH dieters find that they miss conventional pizza after they start their new healthier way of eating. Getting onto the DASH diet doesn't mean you can't enjoy this classic treat, however. This whole-grain, Greek-inspired recipe provides richness with reduced fat ricotta and feta cheese, plus plenty of tasty vegetables. Adding fennel, mint and olive oil gives this recipe an authentic Mediterranean flavor. Once you learn to make these pizzas at home, you won't miss delivery.

Ingredients

10 ounces fresh or frozen spinach
3 ¼ cups low sodium marinara sauce
1 ¼ cups reduced-fat ricotta cheese
1 ¼ cups fresh mint
1 cup fresh fennel
1 whole grain 14 inch pizza crust or equivalent dough
¾ cup feta cheese crumbles
4 plum tomatoes
1 teaspoon strongly-flavored olive oil
1 teaspoon cornmeal
salt substitute and black pepper to taste

Heat a pizza stone or cookie sheet in the oven at 500

degrees Fahrenheit. Sprinkle a pizza peel with cornmeal to prevent sticking. If you are using a pizza crust, follow package instructions to prepare it for topping.

Chop the mint, tomatoes, fennel and spinach. Heat the olive oil in a large skillet to medium-high. Add the chopped fennel and sauté for five minutes, or until slightly translucent. Reduce the heat to medium-low. Drain all water from the spinach and add it to the fennel. Season with black pepper and salt substitute according to your preferences. Place the raw dough on the pizza peel and transfer it to the baking stone or sheet. Cook for 5 minutes at 500 degrees and remove from oven.

Spread the sauce over the pizza crust, then top with the spinach and fennel mixture. Spoon the ricotta in small quantities over the vegetable mixture, but do not try to spread it. Add feta crumbles and bake for another 15 minutes, or until the crust is cooked completely and the edges are lightly browned. Combine the mint and tomatoes in a separate bowl, then sprinkle them over the surface of the pizza before cutting.

Chinese Restaurant Ginger Beef

American-style Chinese food is rarely compatible with the DASH diet, but many people still miss its exciting flavors. The good news is that you can make your own at home, using far less grease, corn syrup and artificial flavors. You'll retain all the best things about restaurant Chinese dishes and avoid the sometimes sticky sauces and high glycemic index. This dish uses thinly-sliced lean beef, heart-friendly oils and fresh ginger to recreate a classic Chinese restaurant favorite.

Ingredients

¾ pound thinly-sliced flank or sirloin steak
1 medium onion
1 pound mushrooms
1 pound broccoli
2 tablespoons peanut oil
1 tablespoon rice vinegar
1 tablespoon fresh ginger
3 cloves fresh garlic
red pepper flakes to taste
salt substitute to taste

In a deep skillet or wok, heat 1 tablespoon of peanut oil on high. Mince the ginger and onion and add to the hot pan, frying for about a minute. Season with salt substitute to taste. Crush the garlic, slice the mushrooms and chop the broccoli. Add 1 teaspoon of garlic and the mushrooms to the pan. Cook for about 2 minutes, stirring throughout, or until the mushrooms soften and the onions become translucent. Add the broccoli and cook for about 3 minutes or until it is bright green and still slightly crisp. Remove the vegetables to a bowl.

Add the remaining tablespoon of peanut oil to the pan and allow it to heat. Add the beef strips and the remaining garlic, cooking for about 2 minutes. Sprinkle in the vinegar and red pepper flakes, followed by the vegetables. Stir to combine and remove from the heat immediately. Serve over short grain brown rice.

Vegetable Medley Pasta Sauce

The DASH diet works best when you reduce the amount of meat in your diet, but many people don't know where to start. This vegetable-based pasta sauce proves that you don't need to have sausage or beef to make a meal special. It uses readily-available dried herbs and fresh vegetables to provide great flavor without the meat. Serve it with your favorite whole grain pasta.

8 ounces canned low-sodium tomato sauce
6 ounces canned low-sodium tomato paste
2 medium zucchini
2 medium fresh tomatoes
2 small onions
3 cloves garlic
2 tablespoons olive oil
1 tablespoon dried oregano
1 tablespoon dried basil
1 teaspoon dried rosemary
1 cup water

Heat the olive oil in a medium-sized skillet. Mince the garlic and onions. Chop the zucchini and tomatoes coarsely. Add all vegetables to the pan and sauté for about 5 minutes over medium-high heat, or until the onions become slightly translucent. Mix the tomato paste and water in a medium bowl until smooth. Add to the pan, along with the tomato sauce and herbs. Cover and reduce the heat to low. Simmer for 45 minutes or until the sauce reaches the desired consistency. Season with salt substitute if desired.

Portabella Mushroom "Burgers"

Not every sandwich you eat on a bun has to be a hamburger. These grilled or pan-seared Portobello mushrooms are marinated in a tasty mixture of vinegar, garlic, cayenne and olive oil, leaving them anything but bland. When you accompany them with the traditional burger toppings, they make the perfect addition to any picnic, potluck or outdoor grilling occasion. Unlike a conventional hamburger, these sandwiches are low in calories, contain almost no fat, and are cholesterol-free.

Ingredients

4 large portabella mushrooms
5 tablespoons balsamic vinegar
2 tablespoons strongly-flavored olive oil
1 tablespoon raw sugar
1 clove garlic
¼ teaspoon sharp paprika

Wash the mushrooms and remove their stems. Place the mushroom caps in an oven-safe glass dish, stem side up. Mince the garlic and combine it with the olive oil, paprika, sugar and vinegar in a separate small bowl. Drizzle this mixture over the mushrooms. Cover and place in the refrigerator for ½ hour. Flip the mushrooms and marinate for an additional ½ hour.

Preheat the broiler or an outdoor grill to moderate heat. If cooking on a grill, lightly coat the rack with cooking spray. Grill or broil the mushrooms on a rack about 6 inches away from the flame, turning periodically and basting with marinade. Transfer to a plate and allow to rest for a few minutes before serving on whole grain buns with lettuce, tomato, onion and low-sodium pickles.

Sides

Baked Macaroni and Cheese

Macaroni and cheese are classic, hearty and comforting, but traditional recipes rely on butter, cream and very large amounts of full fat cheese. The result may be delightful to the taste buds, but it's hard on your arteries. Consider this version instead, which adds ripe tomatoes and reduced fat dairy to produce a baked dish that's delicious without harming your heart. Eat it as a side to an ordinary dinner or with a salad as a light meal all by itself.

Ingredients

2 cups whole grain macaroni
2 cups skim milk
8 ounces reduced fat cheddar cheese
2 fresh tomatoes
2 tablespoons margarine
1 tablespoon flour
1 small onion
1 teaspoon parsley
¼ teaspoon mustard powder
¼ teaspoon black pepper

Grate the cheese and slice the tomatoes and onion very thinly. Boil the macaroni in water according to package instructions, until al dente. Preheat the oven to 400 degrees Fahrenheit and melt margarine over medium-high heat in a sauce pan. Add mustard, flour, pepper and onion, sautéing until the onion becomes translucent. Stir in the milk slowly and cook until smooth and thickened. Add the cheese and stir until just melted. Drain the macaroni and transfer it to a 2 quart baking dish. Pour the cheese mixture over the macaroni and toss gently. Arrange the tomato slices on top of the dish and sprinkle with parsley. Bake for 20 minutes or until the top browns slightly.

Spicy Steamed Eggplant with Peanut Sauce

While most eggplant dishes are best served warm, this unusual side is an excellent cold option for summer. Preparation is quick and easy, and the finished recipe plates up attractively. Make this Asian-inspired dish on hot summer evenings when you don't feel like cooking. Look for long, thin purple Chinese eggplants and serve with cold noodles or rice.

Ingredients

1 ½ pounds eggplant, preferably Asian varieties
2 tablespoons crunchy peanut butter
1 ½ tablespoons low-sodium soy sauce
1 tablespoon apple juice
½ teaspoon chili paste
1 bunch parsley for garnish

Peel the eggplants using a small knife or vegetable peeler, removing the stem from each one. Wrap each eggplant loosely in damp cheesecloth or paper towels and arrange them in a circle around a microwave-safe plate or vegetable steamer. To prepare in the microwave, cook on the high setting for 5 minutes, turning once halfway through cooking. To prepare on the stovetop, steam in a large pot until the eggplant is soft and slightly translucent. Remove the hot eggplants from the microwave or pan and drop them immediately into a bowl of cold water. Remove the cheesecloth or paper towels and cut the vegetables on the diagonal into slices. Arrange on a plate with parsley and chill in the refrigerator.

For the sauce, combine all other ingredients in a small saucepan. Cook, stirring continuously, over medium-low heat until the peanut butter melts and all ingredients are well combined. Spoon over the chilled eggplant and serve.

Braised Spring Vegetables

This hearty combination of winter and new spring vegetables is a great choice when the weather is just beginning to warm. Serve it alongside your favorite meat as a side dish, or eat it on its own as a light lunch or a snack. This recipe is delicious both hot and cold!

Ingredients

1 pound small red, yellow or purple potatoes
1 large carrot
1 medium onion
1 cup green peas, fresh or frozen
½ pound green beans, fresh or frozen
1 clove garlic
½ tablespoon low-sodium soy sauce
1 teaspoon olive oil

Wash all the vegetables and cut the potatoes, carrot and onion into bite size pieces. Top, tail and snap the green beans if you are using fresh vegetables. Mince the garlic. Heat the olive oil in the bottom of a heavy skillet or pan over medium-low heat. Add the potatoes and cook for about 10 minutes or until they begin to brown, stirring occasionally. Add the carrots and cook for another 10 minutes, until both vegetables have begun to tenderize.

Add the sliced onions and garlic. Cook until they become transparent. Fill the pan with water to cover the potatoes and add the green vegetables. Cook until the beans and peas are bright green and tender, but not mushy. Season with soy sauce at the very end of the cooking process.

Rice Pilaf with Saffron

This rice dish is inspired by South Asian pilau, which often include fruit and nuts. Any brown rice will provide the nutty flavor and fiber that are ideal in this recipe, but the best choice is a very dark brown, strong-tasting rice that will provide an appealing contrast for the apricots. Serve this dish hot, as a side for curries or kebabs. If saffron is not available, you can substitute safflower or turmeric for a slightly different flavor.

2 ¼ cups vegetable stock
1 ¼ cups long grain brown rice
¼ cup pistachios
¼ cup dried apricots
3 tablespoons orange juice
1 ½ tablespoons canola, coconut or sunflower oil
¼ teaspoon saffron
salt substitute to taste

Combine the rice, stock and saffron in a medium saucepan. Bring to a boil over high heat. Reduce the heat to low and cover, simmering until the rice has become tender and absorbed all the liquid. Transfer to a large bowl. Combine the orange juice, oil and salt substitute in a small bowl. Pour this mixture over the rice. Chop the apricots. Heat a small skillet to medium and add the fruit and nuts, stirring continuously until the pistachios brown slightly and develop an oily appearance. Toss the fruit and nuts with the flavored rice to mix. Serve right away.

Spicy Garlic Green Beans

Green beans are a classic side dish for all kinds of cuisines, but too many people boil out the nutrients or serve them with copious amounts of butter. Instead of weighing down your beans, celebrate their crisp flavor with this spicy but appealing recipe. Blanching helps set the color and ensures an attractive dish, while a quick sauté with strongly-flavored
ingredients keeps the beans from blending into the background.

Ingredients

1 pound fresh, raw green beans
1 sweet red bell pepper
2 cloves garlic
2 teaspoons extra virgin olive oil
1 teaspoon dark sesame oil
½ teaspoon salt substitute
½ teaspoon chili paste
¼ teaspoon black pepper

Top and tail the beans, removing any strings, and snap them into 2 inch pieces. Bring a large pan of water to a boil over high heat and add the snapped beans. Cook for about 3 minutes, until they become bright green and crisp-tender. Remove the beans from the water and plunge them immediately into a bowl of ice water. Drain and place in a large bowl.

Remove the stem, ribs and seeds from the red bell pepper and cut it into thin strips about 2 inches in length. Heat the olive oil in a large frying pan over medium heat. Add the pepper, stir-frying for about a minute. Add the beans and cook for and additional minute. Crush the garlic and combine with the chili paste, salts substitute and pepper in a small bowl. Add this mixture to the vegetables, stirring to coat. Serve drizzled with sesame oil.

Salads

Spicy Tuna Salad

While the DASH diet emphasizes healthy foods that are lower in fat and cholesterol, that doesn't mean you can't enjoy your favorites. This tuna salad recipe relies on flavorful tomatoes, onions, limes and jalapenos, allowing you to reduce the sodium and cholesterol in other ingredients without losing out on taste.

Ingredients

12 oz. low sodium tuna (about 2 cans)
1/8 cup olive oil or low-fat mayonnaise
1 jalapeno pepper
1 tomato
1 small sweet onion
1 small lime

Drain the water from the tuna and place it in a medium bowl with the mayonnaise. Remove the stem, seeds and ribs from the pepper, dicing it finely. Dice the tomato and the onion. Add the vegetables and lime juice to the bowl and mix thoroughly. Serve with DASH-friendly crackers or bread.

Tabbouleh with Tomatoes

Tabbouleh is a mint-flavored cold salad popular in northern Africa and Western Asia. When made with whole grains, it provides plenty of nutritious fiber, along with refreshing vegetables. The tart flavor of this salad can take a little time to get used to, but it's an extremely welcome change when hot weather comes along. Serve tabbouleh on its own or as a side with kebabs or barbecued meats and vegetables.

Ingredients

½ pound whole grain bulgur wheat
½ pound cucumbers
½ pound fresh tomatoes
3 medium red onions
2 cups flat leaf parsley
½ cup fresh mint
3 lemons
1 tablespoon olive oil
½ teaspoon black pepper

Place the wheat in a large bowl and cover it with water. Soak for one hour or longer, until the grain has absorbed water and plumped. Chop all the vegetables into small cubes or dice and set aside. Drain the bulgur and mix it with the vegetables. Juice the lemons, removing the seeds but reserving the pulp. Add the lemon juice, herbs, oil and pepper to the mixture. Place it in a covered bowl and refrigerate for one to 12 hours. This salad can be stored as is for several days or up to a week with the onions omitted.

Edamame Salad

Fresh, steamed soybeans are known as Edamame in Japan, and are eaten as an appetizer or part of other dishes. When served cold, these beans also make a great salad ingredient. This recipe combines them with cherry tomatoes, fresh mint, dill and scallions. A light oil and vinegar dressing finishes it for a fresh-tasting start to any meal. Try it with a little feta or other salty cheese for added contrast.

Ingredients

½ pound fresh Edamame
1 pint cherry or grape tomatoes
¼ cup red wine vinegar
1 ½ tablespoons extra virgin olive oil
1 scallion
1 small bunch fresh dill weed
1 small bunch fresh mint
¼ teaspoon black pepper

Place the soybeans in a steamer over about an inch of water. Cover and steam for approximately 5 minutes, or until the pods are bright green and the beans are crisp-tender. Rinse with cold water and remove from the pods. Set the beans aside in a medium bowl and refrigerate. Chop the mint and dill finely. Slice the green onion. Cut large cherry tomatoes into halves, leaving small ones whole. Combine tomatoes, green onion, mint and dill in a medium bowl. Mix oil, vinegar and black pepper in a small bowl and pour over the salad. Serve chilled.

Raw Okra Salad

Many people associate okra with slimy boiled preparations or greasy fried food. This unusual member of the mallow family doesn't have to be cooked, however. When sliced carefully and served raw, it has an exciting crispness and lacks any unappealing mucilage. Combine it with spicy mixed salad greens, jicama and sweet peppers for a refreshing salad that's a little outside the usual fare.

Ingredients

1 cup fresh okra
1/3 pound fresh salad greens
1 pound jicama
1 small sweet red bell pepper
4 tablespoons low sodium poppy-seed salad dressing
¼ teaspoon salt substitute
1/4 teaspoon black pepper

Remove the stems from the okra and slice them in half vertically, using a clean, absolutely dry knife. Wipe the knife off between pieces to reduce mucilage production. Remove the stem, seeds and ribs from the pepper and cut it into strips. Peel and slice the jicama into matchsticks. Combine the okra, salad greens, pepper and jicama in a large bowl. Toss gently and season with salt substitute and fresh pepper. Top with poppy-seed dressing and serve immediately.

Tomato-Zucchini Salad with Eggs

Squash and tomatoes are abundant and at their best in the heat of summer, which is the best time to make this refreshing salad. The addition of eggs provides a little more heartiness and allows this dish to act as a light lunch or a starter. For a slightly different flavor, consider using different types of fresh herbs.

Ingredients

2 pounds zucchini
2 pounds ripe tomatoes
6 to 8 eggs
½ cup fresh basil
Dressing:
2 tablespoons extra virgin olive oil
¼ cup red wine vinegar
1 tablespoon fresh parsley
1 teaspoon raw sugar

Combine all dressing ingredients in a glass bowl and mix thoroughly. Set aside. Slice the zucchini and tomatoes into thin rounds. Bring one large and one small pot of water to a boil. Place the eggs in one pot, immediately cover, and reduce heat. Plunge the zucchini rounds into the larger pot for 2 to 3 minutes. Remove from the pot and place immediately in ice water. Drain completely and arrange alternately with the tomato slices on a large plate. Drain the eggs and place them in a bowl of ice water. Peel and slice, arranging the slices on top of the zucchini and tomato rounds. Cover with basil leaves, then drizzle vinegar mixture over the entire platter.

Low Cholesterol Potato Salad

Traditional potato salad is a must at many picnics, but it's loaded with cholesterol, fat and sodium. All of these ingredients can be hazardous for your heart, so many DASH dieters feel as though potato salad is off the menu. This recipe offers much of the same creamy taste and texture, but without the fat and salt. Bring it to your next picnic and no one will ever worry about it being "health food."

Ingredients

1 pound yellow or red waxy potatoes
1 large yellow sweet onion
2 stalks celery
1 large carrot
¼ cup reduced-calorie mayonnaise
2 tablespoons dill weed
2 tablespoons red wine vinegar
1 tablespoon prepared brown mustard

Boil the potatoes in their skins, allow to cool, and dice. Mince the onion and dill weed. Dice the carrot and celery into small pieces. Combine the mayonnaise, mustard, vinegar, pepper and dill in a large bowl. Stir in the vegetables, mixing to coat the pieces completely.

Cover and refrigerate for one hour to overnight to allow the flavors to mingle. Serve chilled.

Soups

Nutrient-packed Kale Soup

The unique, slightly-nutty taste of kale makes this soup an interesting and satisfying starter for any cold season meal, while providing a wide range of healthy vitamins. Adding homemade croutons gives this creamy recipe a hearty crunch without too much fat or too many processed carbohydrates. Plus, their freshness will help them outshine any store-bought option. Enjoy this soup whenever the weather turns chilly and kale is readily available.

Ingredients

6 cups fresh kale leaves
4 cups low sodium broth or stock, preferably vegetable
3 medium red potatoes
1 small white onion
1 tablespoon olive oil
1 tablespoon fresh thyme
1 clove fresh garlic
½ teaspoon black pepper
¼ teaspoon salt substitute
Croutons:

2 cups day old whole grain bread pieces
2 tablespoons olive oil
1 tablespoon fresh thyme
1 tablespoon fresh parsley
1 teaspoon garlic powder

Trim the kale leaves and remove any tough ribs. Chop the onion and the potatoes into small dice. Crush the garlic. Heat 1 tablespoon of olive oil in a heavy pan over medium heat and sauté the chopped onion, crushed garlic and fresh thyme for 7 to 8 minutes or until the onions are transparent. Add the diced potatoes, salt substitute and pepper. Stir well and cook for another 10 minutes or until the potatoes have begun to soften. Remove the cover and add the kale. Cook uncovered for 5 minutes, then add broth, cover and heat for an additional 5 minutes or until the kale becomes bright green and tender. Place half of the soup in a food processor or blender and process until completely smooth. Return this mixture to the saucepan and mix thoroughly.

Croutons: Cut or break bread into pieces approximately ½ inch across. Combine garlic powder, 2 tablespoons olive oil and herbs in a large bowl and add the bread. Toss to coat the outside of the bread but do not allow the oil to soak in. Place croutons on a baking sheet lined with foil and bake at 350 degrees for about 10 minutes or until the outsides are crisp and golden. Cool and use to top bowls of hot soup.

Meatless Lentil Chili

This tasty vegetarian alternative to conventional chili is hearty and flavorful, with bulgur wheat and lentils replacing the usual fatty beef and chili beans. If you're trying to reduce the number of days on which you eat meat, this chili is a great way to start. Serve with diced scallions, low fat sour cream or a DASH-friendly cornbread. For a more interesting chili, substitute red, yellow or black lentils for the traditional brown variety.

Ingredients

3 cups low-sodium vegetable broth
2 cups or one can chopped tomatoes
1 cup bulgur wheat
1 cup dried lentils
1 medium white onion
4 cloves garlic
2 tablespoons canola oil
2 ½ tablespoons chili powder
1 tablespoon cumin powder
½ teaspoon cinnamon
Salt substitute and pepper to taste

Heat the oil to medium-high in a large pot. Mince the onion and garlic, then add them to the pot and cook for

5 minutes, stirring continuously. When the alliums have become slightly translucent, add the wheat and lentils, followed by the broth. Stir to combine, then add the tomatoes and spices. Bring to a boil over high heat, then reduce to low and cover. Simmer for 30 minutes or until the lentils just begin to fall apart. Add salt substitute and pepper to taste and serve hot.

Tangy Carrot Curry

This smooth soup contains plenty of exciting spices, along with protein-rich low fat yogurt and bright, tangy cilantro. The result is an antioxidant-filled dish you'll enjoy with a fresh salad and a slice of homestyle whole-grain bread. For a spicier version, substitute cayenne or Thai peppers for the jalapeno.

Ingredients

5 cups low-sodium vegetable stock
1 pound carrots
1 large yellow onion
1 jalapeno pepper
¼ cup cilantro leaves
¼ cup low fat unsweetened yogurt
2 tablespoons lime or lemon juice
1 tablespoon sunflower oil
1 tablespoon fresh ginger
2 cloves garlic
2 teaspoons Madras curry powder
1 teaspoon black mustard seeds
salt substitute to taste

Heat the olive oil in a large saucepan to medium. Mince the garlic and ginger and chop the onion finely. Add the mustard seed to the oil and allow it to pop, then add the ginger, garlic and onion. Cook for about 5 minutes, stirring continuously, or until the onions become translucent but not brown. Remove the stem, seeds and ribs of the jalapeno and chop it finely, then add to the pan along with the curry powder. Chop the carrots roughly and sauté with the other ingredients for about 3 minutes, or until the seasonings begin to toast. Pour in about half of the stock and bring the whole pot to a boil over high heat. Reduce to medium-low and simmer for about 5 minutes, or until the carrots become tender.

Remove the soup from the pot and place it in a blender or food processor. Process until the liquid is smooth, in batches if necessary, and return to the pan. Stir in the remaining stock and reheat. Add yogurt, cilantro and lime juice, as well as salt substitute to taste. Garnish with additional cilantro and limes before serving.

Cream of Wild Rice Soup with Fennel

Traditional cream of rice soups are extremely comforting, but they're also heavy on butter, cream and refined carbohydrates, making them unsuitable for the DASH diet. Instead, consider this version. It gets its creaminess from white beans and low fat milk and includes vitamin-packed kale and carrots. If wild rice is unavailable in your area, consider substituting any long grain brown rice, such as Basmati, or red rice.

2 cups 1 percent or skim milk
2 cups low-sodium vegetable stock
1 ½ cups kale
1 cup cooked white beans, unsalted
¼ cup wild rice
2 stalks celery
1 large sweet onion
1 large carrot
1 tablespoon fresh parsley
½ tablespoon vegetable oil
1 teaspoon fennel
1 teaspoon black pepper
salt substitute to taste

Place wild rice in a small pot and cover with water. Bring to a boil over high heat, then reduce heat and simmer until the rice has become tender but chewy, or about one hour. Dice the carrot, celery, onion and parsley. Heat the vegetable oil in a large pot over medium heat, then add the onion, carrot, celery and spices. Cook, stirring periodically, until the onions are translucent, the carrots have become slightly tender. Add the parsley, kale and stock. Season with salt substitute to taste.

Combine the milk with the cooked white beans in a blender or food processor. Puree until smooth and add gradually to the soup, stirring continuously. Bring to a simmer and add the cooked rice. Simmer for an additional 30 minutes or until flavors have diffused. Serve with crusty low-sodium bread.

Hearty Turkey Soup

This recipe isn't just a way to use up the leftovers from a big holiday meal, it's also a hearty low-sodium option that includes plenty of healthy winter vegetables. Serve big bowls of this dish with rice or bread as meals on their own, or as a side for lunch or dinner.

Ingredients

Carcass from one turkey
2 quarts low-sodium chicken or vegetable broth
1 quart water
4 large yellow onions
1 large turnip
1 pound carrots
2 cups tomatoes, fresh or canned
2 cups cooked white beans, home-cooked or canned
½ pound light turkey
¼ cup hulled whole barley
1/3 cup fresh parsley
½ teaspoon black pepper
¼ teaspoon thyme
1 bay leaf
salt substitute to taste

Place the turkey carcass in a large stockpot with the

broth and water. Bring to a boil over high heat. Chop one onion into quarters and add to the pot. Reduce the heat, cover, and allow the pot to simmer for an hour. Remove all solids from the pot and place the stock in the refrigerator for 2 hours to overnight. Skim off any fat from the cooled broth and discard. Return the broth to its original pot.

Chop the carrots, turnip, tomatoes and remaining onions and add them to the broth. Add the bay leaf, beans, barley, herbs and spices to the mixture, stirring to combine. Cut the turkey meat into bite-sized chunks and add to the pot. Bring the entire mixture to a simmer, then cover and allow to cook for an hour or until all the vegetables have softened. Serve immediately.

DASH Diet 5-Day Sample Menu

Deciding how to eat on the DASH diet plan can be tricky if you're not used to dealing with its rules. Here's a quick 5-day sample menu using some recipes from this book to help you get started. There's no reason to stick to just this menu, however. You can mix and match the recipes or use foods of your own. Just make sure that you stick to the guidelines set forth earlier in this book and it'll be hard to go wrong!

Day 1

Breakfast: Fresh orange juice, whole grain toast with low-sugar fruit spread, DASH-Friendly Oatmeal

Lunch: Tangy Carrot Curry, fresh vegetable crudités, brown rice
Snack: almonds, hazelnuts or cashews, fresh peach or nectarine

Dinner: Blackened Beef, Tabbouleh with Tomatoes, Chewy Fruit Bars

Day 2

Breakfast: Healthy Homemade Granola, fresh strawberries, skim milk

Lunch: Miso-Marinated Cod, Edamame Salad, hot green tea

Snack: fat-free, low-sugar yogurt, graham crackers

Dinner: Chinese Restaurant Ginger Beef, brown rice, fresh oranges

Day 3

Breakfast: Toasted Breakfast Sandwich, fresh orange juice

Lunch: Spicy Tuna Salad on whole grain bread with lettuce and tomato,
Sugar Free Agua Fresca

Snack: Pretzels, raisins, sunflower seeds

Dinner: Feta-ricotta Greek Pizza, lettuce hearts, olives

Day 4

Breakfast: Peanut Butter and Banana Smoothie, whole

grain bagel with light cream cheese

Lunch: Meatless lentil chili, low-sodium cornbread, tomatoes, low-fat sour cream

Snack: Vegetable Sushi

Dinner: Simple Grilled Chicken, Braised Spring Vegetables, vanilla wafers

Day 5

Breakfast: Chewy Fruit Bars, Spicy, Sweet and Tangy Herbal Tea

Lunch: Tomato-Zucchini Salad with Eggs, whole grain pasta with
Vegetable Medley Pasta Sauce

Snack: apple, whole grain crackers

Dinner: Portabella Mushroom "Burgers", Low Cholesterol Potato Salad, low fat frozen yogurt

Modifying the 5-Day Meal Plan

Because every person has different calorie requirements, it's hard to say how much you'll need to eat of these foods at any given meal. If you take a little time to look at your activity level and personal habits, you'll have an easier time choosing the right calorie level for you. The main DASH diet offers 1,200, 1,600, 2,000 and 2,400 calorie options for various amounts of activity and various metabolisms. In general, if you're hoping to lose weight, consider choosing a calorie goal that's one rung lower than the one you need to maintain.

That means that if you're relatively active but overweight, you could move down from the 2,000 calories that you probably need to stay at your current weight, choosing a 1,600 calorie per day diet, instead. You'd aim to get the same 4 to 5 servings of fruits and vegetables per day, as well as the same 3 to 4 servings of low fat dairy, nuts and beans, but you'd limit your meat consumption to just 5 ounces per day and cut back on fats and sweets. It may take a little while to figure things out, but you can help it along by doubling up on low calorie vegetables, fruits and non-fat dairy while limiting meat, cheese and grain consumption.

Conclusion

The average American diet is high in unhealthy fried food and high-fat meat and dairy sources, as well as too much sugar. The result, for many people, is skyrocketing blood pressure and an increased risk of heart disease and stroke. If you're worried that your health could be at risk, it's time to take steps.

That means moving to the DASH diet and avoiding unhealthy foods in favor of rich, flavorful options that are low in fat and high in vitamins. While it's true that the adjustment period may take a little longer than you expect, all these recipes will help you make the transition. You won't miss the fat or extra sugar! Just focus on the healthy foods that you can eat and work to make fruits and vegetables a regular part of your routine. Your heart and your waistline will thank you.

www.ingramcontent.com/pod-product-compliance
Ingram Content Group UK Ltd.
Pitfield, Milton Keynes, MK11 3LW, UK
UKHW021904240426
12048UKWH00044B/632